TEDDYBEARS TO BOMBS

Dr. E. Thomas Carroll II, M.A. LMHC

authorHOUSE®

AuthorHouse™
1663 Liberty Drive
Bloomington, IN 47403
www.authorhouse.com
Phone: 1-800-839-8640

First published by AuthorHouse   06/10/2011

ISBN: 978-1-4490-6925-4 (sc)
ISBN: 978-1-4490-6926-1 (hc)
ISBN: 978-1-4490-6927-8 (e)

Library of Congress Control Number: 2011909155

Printed in the United States of America

Any people depicted in stock imagery provided by Thinkstock are models,
and such images are being used for illustrative purposes only.
Certain stock imagery © Thinkstock.

This book is printed on acid-free paper.

Contents

INTRODUCTION   VII

CHAPTER 1. IN THE BEGINNING   1

CHAPTER 2. WHEN YOU WERE BORN   2

CHAPTER 3. THE ADHD CONNECTION   4

CHAPTER 4. INFANCY AND COMMUNICATION   6

    Infancy (Birth-12 Months)   10

CHAPTER 5. THE YOUNGER YEARS   15

    Younger Years (1-3 Years)   15

    Early Childhood (3-5 Years)   16

    Middle Childhood (6-10 Years)   17

CHAPTER 6. THE ADOLESCENT STAGE OF DEVELOPMENT   19

    Adolescence (11-18 Years)   19

CHAPTER 7. BEING PASSIVE AND LEARNING TO ADAPT   20

CHAPTER 8. LETS GET EVEN   23

CHAPTER 9. LEARNING HOW TO COMMUNICATE   25

    What is Assertiveness?   25

    Selfishness and Aggressiveness   28

    What Assertiveness Will Not Do   28

    Learning to Become More Assertive   30

CHAPTER 10. SELF-ESTEEM   31

    THE TRUE MEANING OF SELF-ESTEEM   32

    User Submitted Quotations.   35

CHAPTER 11. LEARNING HOW TO FIT   40

CHAPTER 12. AGGRESSIVE, WHAT IS IT?   41

    How angry are you   41

CHAPTER 13. UNDERSTANDING ANGER   46

CHAPTER 14. MARITAL CONFLICT   50

Dealing with the "enemy of lovers"　　　　　　　　　52

Trying to get our way　　　　　　　　　　　　　54

Finding better ways to resolve anger in relationships　　55

A long-term concern; an important problem　　　　58

1. "swallowers " or repressor-suppressor, or　　　61

2. "exploders " or hotheaded expressers.　　　　61

Level I: Anger or aggression-control methods that focus on

simple behavior and thoughts.　　　　　　　　62

　　Explain yourself and understand others.　　62

　　Develop better ways of behaving.　　　　63

CHAPTER 15.　　REMOTE CONTROL　　　　68

CHAPTER 16.　　THE STORY　　　　　　72

CHAPTER 17.　　THE TOOL BOX　　　　77

CHAPTER 18.　　THE TEDDYBEAR TO BOMB STORY　80

Chapter 1: Welcome to average town　　　　80

Chapter 2: The really cool teacher　　　　81

Chapter 3: Skipping homeroom　　　　　82

Chapter 4: Getting to Homeroom Early　　83

Chapter 5: Learning The Secret　　　　85

Chapter 6: The New Secret　　　　　89

Chapter 7: Pushing Buttons　　　　93

Chapter 8: The Habit　　　　　　96

Chapter 9: Realizing　　　　　　98

Chapter 10: Slipping　　　　　104

Chapter 11: Helping Others　　　105

Chapter 12: The Success Gang　　107

REFERENCES　　　　　　　　108

INTRODUCTION

Our behaviors, emotions, spirituality, aptitudes, internal chemistry and much more, began as far back as when the first man walked the earth. Biblically speaking, was that Adam and Eve? Or one of the other humans as stated in the Bible in Genesis? Yes, in the time of Genesis, there were other people on Earth and not just Adam and Eve. We will examine some of the aspects regarding growth and development, our personality formation, our inborn Temperament, our behaviors, emotions, fears, learning abilities, and how we are affected by our environments and how we affect our environments. We begin learning from our environment before our birth and before our parents, too. We are going to begin our journey at the time of conception, or just a little before, and follow some of the many paths that directly affect who we become! This journey will also point out how to change negative paths into positive goals, and how to learn self-control to help become more successful.

Chapter 1
IN THE BEGINNING
Who Are You

You must be a somewhat unique and intelligent person from age 5 and up, because you have started reading this fantastic book. You have an interest in finding out what makes you a teddy bear or a time bomb, non-assertive person, Mr. Milktoast; bully, mean, nasty, fighting, aggressive or passive, wimpy, whiney, pushed around, or pushing around another person.

This book contains proven effective methods and interventions that can help the passive or aggressive person alter their personal ways of dealing with situations within, school, family, job, and community, live more productive, fulfilling lives, and allow you to learn how to continue controlling you.

You may be reading this book to find out how to help someone that you love or care about, or you are a counselor and want to help one of or a group of your clients with one of the most common but difficult problems that exist today in our society.

You may also want to find out why you are either passive or aggressive.

You may also want to know how **you and only you** can change to be a more consistent, get-along, and get-your-own-way (some of the time) person.

You must have a desire to fit into the world around you, your community, job, school, or family. Fitting in will be discussed later on in the book under its own heading.

You don't need to pick whether you are passive or aggressive just quite yet. Some people are passive-aggressive, too; what a twist that can be! All people have some of both traits of being passive or being aggressive in our internal makeup. At times we can be the caveman and thump our chests and go out into the world to fight and conquer anything that gets in our way, both guys and girls alike. At other times we may want to sit alone and go along with anyone who is around us in a most passive way. You may have a desire to give in because . . .

WHY; why will be thoroughly explained later.

1

Chapter 2

WHEN YOU WERE BORN

The only thing we know when we are born is to get angry about almost everything. At this stage of development, we must learn to love and be loved by our caregivers. Our most basic need of survival and safety are just emerging. We want for us and only us, we desire all of the most primary comforts until we learn more. Some of these thought patterns came to us prior to our birth in the formation of our individual and unique temperament. As the KJV Bible states in Psalms 139, 13-15: "[13] For thou hast possessed my reins: thou hast covered me in my mother's womb. [14] I will praise thee; for I am fearfully *and* wonderfully made: marvellous *are* thy works; and *that* my soul knoweth right well. [15] My substance was not hid from thee, when I was made in secret, *and* curiously wrought in the lowest parts of the earth. "

Think back about when you were born or when a sibling or friend's baby was born and how the child reacted to the world situations ... Picture this in your mind: you are now a fetus, surrounded by warm water; all your immediate needs are met. You have all that you need and desire, the warmth, the strange sounds that you hear from outside your womb home. Sometimes the sounds are peaceful as you listen to music coming from a radio or musical instrument or mom singing in the shower, but sometimes you hear loud mean sounds and then you feel bouncing around and thumping. Your heart races as your internal chemistry starts with Adrenaline and Cortosol. Your awareness is heightened, and now you start to feel uncomfortable as you kick and punch within your womb home. A little while later, quiet noises are heard and new chemicals start to calm you down as the Dopamine and Serotonin are being sent to your little brain. Then, one day around the 40th week of gestation, you start to feel pushed around and bothered by more chemicals that increase your awareness and heighten your desire to move. And all of a sudden you feel your head being squashed and your nose pushed into your face, and being grabbed by hands and turned around, your shoulders hurt from being bent around, and then bright lights, VERY BRIGHT LIGHTS, and COLD AIR, and now you have a very heavy feeling as someone grabs your feet and ankles while suspending you upside down. Then something is jammed into your right nostril and then the left nostril sucking like it seems to be sucking your brains out, and then the thing is jammed down your throat and more sucking feelings, and you scream for your life, yelling, getting as mad and angry as you have ever felt. Then your back hits a hard flat surface, nothing like floating in water and, all of a sudden, a very sharp pain, as one of those enormous creatures stabs a needle into your heel. You scream again, fighting for your life as nothing is like it had been, air is cold, stabbing pains; you have never felt this much rage and fear. Anger is the one emotion that all animals use as their first tool in their toolbox of skills that, for the most part, immediately helps to survive.

Now you can probably see how you began from the beginning, and all of the information and life experiences really add to how our individual personalities or masks are developed. But, there is more to come in the next chapter.

Chapter 3
THE ADHD CONNECTION

Another scenario: as you're forming within the confines of the womb, mom loves to drink coffee and, as the caffeine passes the placental barrier, you too get to have your morning cup of coffee. Your brain surges with adrenaline and other stimulants causing you to have a heightened awareness of your world. After a very short period of time, you become used to having coffee every morning with mom as she drinks her three or four cups of "Joe". Then, when you are born, HOW MANY moms PUT COFFEE IN THE BABY'S BOTTLE?

The first few days after being born, the withdrawal symptoms of headache, fatigue, lethargy, and tiredness continue for a lifetime as you are a caffeine addict from before birth. Your brain gives off beta waves in this time of sluggish functioning, just like when we feel we need to take a nap. This sluggishness with brain activity will continue through a lifetime and never cease until we have our daily stimulants. In the 1930's, coffee became a beverage of choice and, in the 1950's and 1960's, it became a trend that moms and dads drank all over the United States. And now in the 1990's and 2005, coffee stores are all competing as coffee is the United States' most popular drink, or a soft drink that has caffeine in it is the second choice. And then there are HIGH ENERGY drinks that have too much sugar, ginkgo baloba, and caffeine too.

Have you ever heard of ADHD (Attention Deficit Hyperactivity Disorder)? The children in the 1970's first learned that they may have a disorder, and the cause was unknown. In the 1990's, almost 50% of all children have ADHD. And we continued to wonder where and why all of a sudden lots of people had ADHD and never had it before. Human beings require their brains to operate in the alpha stage to give us enough brain energy to concentrate and use self-control doing away with immature impulsive behaviors. In the 1970's, physicians started using Adderall and Ritalin to help those children's brains reach the Alpha Brain Wave stage of awareness. Today in the year 2006, children are most commonly diagnosed with a level of ADHD due to their Beta Brain Wave emissions, lack of self-control, impulsive behaviors, twitching, jumping around, off-task behaviors, not paying attention, failing to complete tasks, and forgetting what the tasks were that had to be done, like homework. Today there is an epidemic of caffeine abuse and ADHD children in America.

You may be asking "So what does this have to do with me?" ADHD is one of the most common diagnoses in the United States of America, and it most likely has always existed and in other countries, too! Self-control is of the utmost behavior to learn, and there are no classes or trainings that have existed before this book.

Chapter 4

INFANCY AND COMMUNICATION

Back to the infancy stage. The infant that is just born desires to communicate. They don't know how to speak English, Spanish, or any other language, but they do know infant communication skills like crying and screaming. The new infant wants to be changed because it is uncomfortable and hurts; what does the infant do? He cries and balls his tiny fists in anger. According to the KJV Bible anger is "²⁶ Be ye angry, and sin not: let not the sun go down upon your wrath: ²⁷ Neither give place to the devil. ²⁸ Let him that stole steal no more: but rather let him labour, working with *his* hands the thing which is good, that he may have to give to him that needeth. ²⁹ Let no corrupt communication proceed out of your mouth, but that, which is good to the use of edifying, that it may minister grace unto the hearers. ³⁰ And grieve not the Holy Spirit of God, whereby ye are sealed unto the day of redemption. ³¹ Let all bitterness, and wrath, and anger, and clamour, and evil speaking, be put away from you, with all malice: ³² And be ye kind one to another, tenderhearted, forgiving one another, even as God for Christ's sake hath forgiven you."

The infant is at the mercy of anyone that can help it. Think about it; when the infant is hungry, what does he do? He screams and cries to get attention and is angry and, if left alone, will continue to scream and cry and get angrier until someone or something takes care of his basic need. The reason I use the word **something** in this sentence is to point out that it may not be mom or dad or big brother or sister that will be the one to take care of his need. Do you remember hearing about the boy who was found in the woods by a wolf pack, and the mother wolf raised the child to be a fine puppy? The mother wolf took the infant in as if it was its own, and cared for the infant. The wolf mother cleaned it, kept it warm, and fed the infant as if it was one of its own puppies. This human infant learned to trust the caregiver, and she was the most important being in his life. Some years later, when the child had grown up, he was found by people and removed from the natural woods setting that all wolves live in, and placed in a shelter within a town. At that point, the child was being transferred into human civilization and had to learn the social skills of humans; however, he was doing just fine as a wolf; he thought so, anyway.

This child was given everything that it needed: discipline, love, warmth, affection, food, and anything else he needed by the wolf pack and his mother wolf. We all can learn to be successful and attach and bond to another person but only up to approximately the age of 24 months. After 24 months of age, we have a difficult time learning to trust our caregiver if we have not learned to TRUST. Trust and mistrust are learned by the infant from birth to approximately 24 months of age.

Even though you can't go back and change your knowledge of trust vs. mistrust, how well did you learn it? The future development and success of those infants that you come in contact with as a caregiver are up to you.

Recently, I was speaking to a new mother, and she said that she was a daycare baby who was in day-care from one week old until she started school. She said that her parents were never together as they parted ways before her birth. Her mother had to work all of the time, and she was in a daycare setting throughout her infancy. I asked her if her mother checked out the daycare center to learn if the caregivers had been employed there for a long time and almost never were replaced. She didn't know, and asked why. I told her that most parents think that their infant is okay if care-giving is done by a variety of people, and what would it matter who feeds the infant, who is the one that plays with the infant, who is the caregiver that meets the immediate needs of the infant? However, it is very important during the first year to have the same consistent caring and loving caregiver so that the infant can learn to trust that caregiver for all of their needs. It is the only time that trust can be learned, and that the trust level of achievement is the one thing that will affect their job stability, learning ability, marriage and relationship stability, and other stable, continual growth factors of being a successful adult.

The era has changed, and people have grown from the prehistoric man through the era of mechanization, and have continued on into the 21st century, a time from hunting and barbaric styles of survival and little communication into the current days of microwaves, televisions, computers, fast foods, cell phones and little personal communication.

In the beginning of our lives and throughout our lifetimes, we require having many needs met and obtained. Those are as follows as Maslow stated in his theory of the Human Hierarchy of Needs:

1.   **Biological and Physiological needs:air, food, drink, shelter, warmth, sex, sleep, etc.**
2.   2. **Safety needs:** protection from elements, security, order, law, limits, stability, etc.
3.   3. **Belongingness and Love needs:** - work group, family, affection, relationships, etc.
4.   4. **Esteem needs:** - self-esteem, achievement, mastery, independence, status, dominance, prestige, managerial responsibility, etc.
5.   5. **Self-Actualization needs:** - realizing personal potential, self-fulfillment, seeking personal growth and peak experiences.

Maslow's Hierarchy of Needs states:

1.   That we must satisfy each need in turn, starting with the first that deals with the most obvious needs for survival itself.
2.   Only when the lower-order needs of physical and emotional well-being are satisfied are we concerned with the higher-order needs of influence and personal development.
3.   Conversely, if the things that satisfy our lower-order needs are swept away, we are no longer concerned about the maintenance of our higher-order needs.

First examine those Basic Safety Needs of the Prehistoric Cave Man Era.

Biological and physiological needs of the cave- man and cavewoman

The caveman and/or cavewoman needs are: air, food, drink, shelter, warmth, sex, sleep, etc. Relationships were formed by a cavewoman and cave-man in the simplest forms of human bonding. The man was chosen by the woman because of his being smart and well built, showing that he could hunt and catch food in addition to his ability to protect himself from hungry lions and tigers and other cavemen. Food: fresh killed animals, nuts and berries that the cavewoman found on the ground. These skills of hunting and gathering were performed by the two genders appropriately: the male hunted, and the female, being smaller built, gathered berries and nuts while staying close to the cave (shelter). As God stated in the KJV Bible for man and woman to replenish the earth:

Gen 1:28 And God blessed them, and God said unto them, be fruitful, and multiply, and replenish the earth, and subdue it: and have dominion over the fish of the sea, and over the fowl of the air, and over every living thing that moveth upon the earth. In the caveman times, relationships were formed without very much communication. Pictures were drawn on the ground in the sand, and cave pictures were drawn on the cave walls as we have seen in history books. The cavemen would adventure off into the wilderness to hunt and bring back meat to the cavewoman and family for them to eat.

Safety needs

While the caveman would be away, the woman and children would scurry around picking up berries and nuts to eat while staying close to the cave for protection and safety. Upon his return with the killed animal, the family would feast and feel safer within their organized cave dwelling. The caveman was the leader of the home, and kept order and safety precautions for his cavewoman and cave- children.

Belongingness and Love needs

Before the cave child was born, just like today, the couple would spend countless hours being close and experiencing each other in kind, and meeting the emotional needs of each other. Mankind yesteryear and today continues to have the NEED for closeness, love and emotional ties.

Esteem needs

The caveman had the need to be recognized as a good provider and safekeeper. The cavewoman had the need to be recognized by her partner as the helpmate, gatherer of nuts and berries, supplier of the basic emotional needs of the children, and the caveman.

Self-Actualization needs

In the day of cave people, self-actualization may have been the cave family with the most skins, most food to eat, having the best health, more rocks to throw, bigger clubs to beat animals and having more of everything they needed to survive.

Taking all of the above into consideration and putting it into the perspective of today's life circumstances, not much has changed. The man and woman go out into the business world to hunt and gather money to supply the food and shelter for the family. They have cell phones and computers to communicate with others. Everything is faster paced, and where are the children? Being kept in a day-care center by some usually unknown person who provides questionable care, and is teaching the basic concepts to our infants.

Erikson's eight stages of psychosocial development incorporates a journey from infancy through adulthood; when successful,will live a healthy, happy life. Each stage has it's crisis that must be resolved or it will manifest itself in a later time in the future as a problem. The challenges of growing psychosocially are typical of most humans.

Infancy (Birth-12 Months)

- Psychosocial Crisis: Trust vs. Mistrust

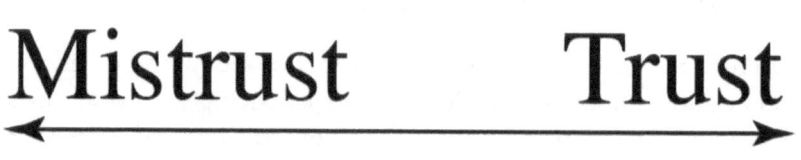

Developing trust is the first task of the ego, and it is never complete. This is the period of development where the infant learns about hope and the act of bonding while becoming emotionally bound to the caregiver. When successful, the child will let mother out of sight without anxiety and rage because she has become an intrinsic certainty as well as an extrinsic predictability. The balance of trust with mistrust depends largely on the quality of the maternal relationship.

We can look at the balance of trust vs. mistrust as a sliding scale of competency or achievement in attachment and hope.

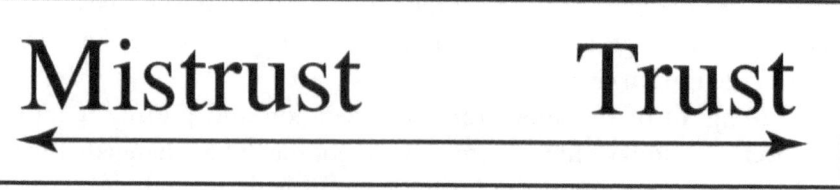

Main question asked: "Is my world predictable and supportive?"
- Central Task: Receiving care
- Positive Outcome: Trust in people and the environment
- Ego Quality: Hope!
- Definition: Enduring belief that one can attain one's deep and essential wishes
- Developmental Task: Social attachment; maturation of sensory, perceptual, and motor functions; primitive causality
- Significant Relations: Maternal parent

The concept of trust vs. mistrust is present throughout an individual's entire life. Therefore, if the concept is not addressed, taught and handled properly during infancy (when it is first introduced), an individual may be negatively affected, and never fully immerse themselves in the world. The formation of trust vs. mistrust must occur between birth and 26 months of age. If an infant learns to mistrust (having little or no consistent love, affection, care, basic survival safety needs being met), they will develop hopelessness, and have a degree of Reactive Attachment Disorder. Reactive Attachment Disorder is a life-long problem that will NEVER be resolved. For example, a person may hide themselves from the outside world, and be unable to form healthy and long-lasting relationships with others or even themselves. If an individual does not learn to trust themselves, others and the world, they may lose the virtue of hope. If a person loses their belief in hope, they will struggle with overcoming hard times and failures in their lives, and may never fully recover from them preventing them from learning and maturing into the person they were meant to be, if the concept of trust vs. mistrust was properly learned, understood and used in all aspects of their life.

COMMUNICATION STYLE:

The neonate or infant communicates immediately at the time of birth using the only skill that they know: crying or being quiet. Crying is the infant's method of communicating to the caregiver (mom, dad, big brother, big sister, daycare worker, etc.): I am angry, LOOK AT ME, PAY ATTENTION RIGHT NOW AND TAKE CARE OF MY IMMEDIATE SAFETY NEEDS and you, the caregiver, must listen and interpret what that exact need is at that time.

ANGER:

The first emotion that infants are able to understand and communicate is anger. Anger is necessary, needed, it is the major method for survival. As we know, all infants are totally helpless and incapable of doing anything for themselves. The infant is totally, 100% DEPENDENT ON THE CAREGIVER. THEY HAVE NO ABILITY TO BE INDEPENDENT AT ALL.

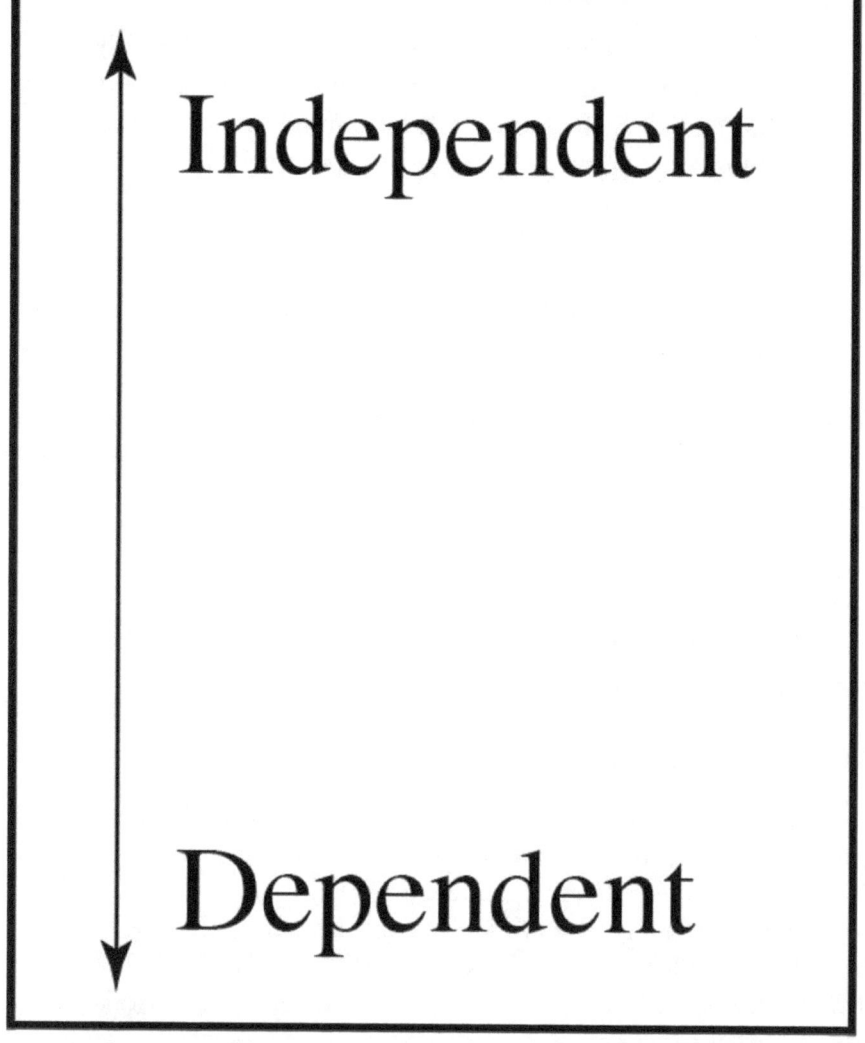

At the time of birth, the infant only knows the things that it has learned while being inside the womb. He knows that there are times of being satisfied; times of being distressed when he hears loud arguing and the mother's adrenaline increases due to fear (the fight or flight syndrome); he knows the sound and sight of warm light and soft music playing and mom's emission of hormones like dopamine and serotonin that make the infant feel drowsy and relaxed. The fetus is exposed to almost everything that the mother experiences or ingests. Many things cross the placental barrier, like prescription drugs, alcohol, illegal substances, herbs, caffeine, nicotine, etc. These drugs that cross the barrier affect the fetus and its growth in many areas including the brain; future adaptation to his world is greatly affected. For example, the fetus that is constantly exposed to caffeine will become addicted to caffeine just like the mom is addicted. Its brain will become addicted to the stimulant and figure out that this extra stimulation is necessary for paying attention and being alert. After the child is born, it may show withdrawal from the drug, caffeine, and in later developmental stages be diagnosed with (ADHD) Attention Deficit Hyperactivity Disorder.

During the first few weeks, the infant learns many things from its new environment. The infant is learning to look and gaze at objects that are very close to them as all infants are nearsighted and far away objects are blurry and out of focus.

If an infant has learned to trust or some varying degree of trusting within those 24 months, then he can continue to trust for an entire lifetime. If not, then that person will grow up mistrusting and doubting all of his relationships; i.e., working relationships, partnerships, lovers, children, God, etc.

The only thing that the person who has a major amount of mistrust can do is to learn to adapt to the varying situations and apply a learned behavior to make the best of the situation, otherwise he will jump from relationship to relationship for an entire lifetime. I know many people around me that have some of these same problems, that grow up having problems with their parents, continue to have problems with their employment relationships - almost any type of situation that they are subjected to within their lives. This creates major problems of stability, and leads them to a life of misery and depression.

During this development stage, the infant is learning how to communicate with words. The words that they learn are from their surroundings. As they hear mom and dad or brother or sister, etc., they learn to speak words from those people they hear. They also begin to improve on the emotional and body language that they learned while in the womb.

During the first two years of your development, you learned to use the beginning of communications and your work toward INDEPENDENCE. You had learned to Trust or Mistrust your environment and caregiver, and have a Feeling of Safety or not as you were working on fulfilling those personal biological and physiological needs. Your life-long pursuit toward becoming more Independent and Self-Actualizing was the major mission in your life. Self-Esteem and Independence have a very close relationship as when one is low the other usually follows. When Self-Esteem is low, it brings the feelings of Independence down as anger usually follows suit and makes the communication skills revert to the very dependent style by displaying anger and temper tantrums (just like the 2-year-old). When biological and physiological needs are not met, you will also revert to anger and dependent skills as you will want what you want and need to have those immediate things that will keep you safe and feeling good, like food, shelter, air, water, etc.

The great thing about being a human is that, when we do not have the opportunity to fulfill our development goal at the age we are first introduced to it, we can go back at a later age and resolve some or all of those issues with the exception of the beginning stage of Trust vs. Mistrust. The Trust vs. Mistrust stage is developed from birth to 26 months old, and nobody can go back and fix that developmental issue at another time.

Now we are going to look at the next stage of living and development. And, if you have not been successful in that stage, you may have a tendency to return to the prior Trust vs. Mistrust stage and move through all of the other stages to the present stage of your life's development.

Chapter 5

THE YOUNGER YEARS

Younger Years (1-3 Years)

- Psychosocial Crisis: Autonomy vs. Shame & Doubt

Shame and Doubt   Autonomy

$\longleftarrow\!\!\!\!\!\longrightarrow$

If denied autonomy, the child will turn against his/her urges to manipulate and discriminate. Shame develops with the child's self-consciousness. Doubt has to do with having a front and back - a "behind" subject to its own rules. Leftover doubt may become paranoia. The sense of autonomy fostered in the child and modified as life progresses serves the preservation in economic and political life of a sense of justice.

- Main question asked, Can I do it by myself, or will I always need assistance? This question becomes important with the child and toilet training, and how the parents react to the child's newfound independence.
- Central Task: Imitation
- Positive Outcome: Pride in self; Assertion of will in the face of danger
- Ego Quality: Will
- Definition: Determination to exercise free choice and self-control
- Developmental Task: Locomotion; Fantasy play; Language development; Self-control
- Significant Relations: Parents

During this stage, toddlers learn more communication skills from their surroundings. The toddler may say those words most frequently said within ear range, especially those short four-letter words that are easily pronounced. Those words are also the ones that the parents do not want the toddler to repeat in front of other adults. Have you ever heard the mom or dad say things like, I DON'T KNOW WHERE THEY HEARD THAT WORD!?

Communication skills are being developed right along with body language as they both come together as a package. When toddlers are around or exposed to domestic violence, anger problems, arguing, fighting, etc., it is all natural to them to learn to expand their anger (that they knew at birth) and adapt it to the most prominent circumstances.

Early Childhood (3-5 Years)

- Psychosocial Crisis: Initiative vs. Guilt

Initiative adds to autonomy the quality of undertaking, planning, and attacking a task for the sake of being active and on the move. The child feels guilt over the goals contemplated and the acts initiated in exuberant enjoyment of new locomotive and mental powers. The castration complex occurring in this stage is due to the child's erotic fantasies. A residual conflict over initiative may be expressed as hysterical denial that may cause the repression of the wish or the abrogation of the child's ego: paralysis and inhibition, or overcompensation and showing off. The Oedipal stage results not only in oppressive establishment of a moral sense restricting the horizon of the permissible, but also sets the direction towards the possible and the tangible that permits dreams of early childhood to be attached to goals of an active adult life.

- Main question asked: Am I good or am I bad?
- Central Task: Identification

- Positive Outcome: Able to initiate activities and enjoy learning
- Ego Quality: Purpose
- Definition: Courage to imagine and pursue valued goals
- Developmental Task: Sex-role identification; Early moral development; Self-esteem; Group Play; Egocentrism
- Significant Relations: Basic family

After this stage, one may use the whole repertoire of previous modalities, modes, and zones for industrious, identity-maintaining, intimate, legacy-producing, despair-countering purposes.

More communication skills are learned and experienced during this time. Who teaches those toddlers and children? The daycare workers, moms and dads, brothers and sisters, other children, peers, the pastor of the church we attend, and the next-door neighbors are all teaching, and they don't know it and aren't aware that they are doing it.

Middle Childhood (6-10 Years)

- Psychosocial Crisis: Industry vs. Inferiority

```
┌─────────────────────────────────────────┐
│  Inferiority      Industry               │
│  ◄─────────────────────────────────────► │
└─────────────────────────────────────────┘
```

To bring a productive situation to completion is an aim that gradually supersedes the whims and wishes of play. The fundamentals of technology are developed. To lose the hope of such "industrious" association may pull the child back to the more isolated, less conscious familial rivalry of the Oedipal time.

- Main question asked: Am I successful at what I do or am I worthless? How a child does at school becomes important in development
- Central Task: Education
- Positive Outcome: Acquire skills for and develop competence in work, Enjoy achievement

- Ego Quality: Competence
- Definition: Free exercise of skill and intelligence in completion of tasks
- Developmental Task: Friendship, skill-learning, self-evaluation, team playthings.
- **Significant Relations: School**

Chapter 6

THE ADOLESCENT STAGE OF DEVELOPMENT

Adolescence (11-18 Years)

- Psychosocial Crisis: Identity vs. Role Confusion

The adolescent is newly concerned with how they appear to others. Ego identity is the accrued confidence that the inner sameness and continuity prepared in the past are matched by the sameness and continuity of one's meaning for others as evidenced in the promise of a career. The inability to settle on a school or occupational identity is disturbing.

- Main question asked: Who am I? Where am I going in life? An identity crisis generally happens at this stage because of the changes in an individual. Those changes reflect both physical and cognitive maturation.
- Central Task: Peer group, Cliques
- Positive Outcome: A strong group identity, ready to plan for the future
- Ego Quality: Loyalty
- Definition: Ability to freely pledge and sustain loyalty to others
- Developmental Task: Physical maturation, Emotional development, Membership in peer group, Sexual relationships
- **Significant Relations: Peer groups**

Chapter 7

BEING PASSIVE
AND
LEARNING TO ADAPT

Passive, What Is It?

Passive, according to Funk and Wagnall's dictionary, means "acted upon or receiving impressions from external agents or causes; being the object rather than the subject of action; moved by or as by external force or influence. In a state of rest or quiescence; not vitally or mentally active; unresponsive. Unresisting; submissive; passive obedience. Not provided with, or not making use of, motive power. Not bearing interest: said of bonds which yield the holder a profit or benefit while no rate percent is named; having reference to a debt which, by agreement, is non-interest-bearing; of the nature of liability." According to the Psychiatric Dictionary means "one of the several modalities of adaptation. For example, it is possible for the organism to adapt itself to its environment by going either forward to meet it or backward to escape it. The first procedure would be termed the modality of activity in adaptive maneuvers, while the latter would be termed the modality of passivity.

In transference neurosis, the consequences of inhibition of the modality of activity may find the organism simply abandoning this modality and falling back upon the modality of passivity. In traumatic neurosis, however, the modality of passivity cannot be resorted to when activity is inhibited since it is impossible for the organism to remain completely passive to the outer world. One can retreat from an inhibiting person, but complete retreat from the inhibiting forces of the outer world is impossible short of death."

"Being the object rather than the subject", in Funk and Wagnall's definition, the passive person allows the subject (the other person or persons) to treat them like the object or possession. The passive person gives in to any demand placed upon them by the other person almost all of the time. This passive person almost never gets their way, has ideas of their own, but never voices what they are.

The passive person is the boy or girl who is just one of the guys who does anything the guys want to do. Or he or she is the person at the very back of the line following passively along with whatever the group leader has decided, no matter what that is. This type of person is controlled by the influences or external forces of others rather than by their individual preferences. The passive person blindly follows along, oftentimes getting in trouble or engaging in events that are unwanted by their inner-self.

The passive person often thinks back about the events of the day and how their day progressed, and wonders why they became involved with the activity that they became involved with. They wonder and postulate how it would be different if they would have had a say in the activity. They think that the next time they will act differently and speak up and say something about what they are going to do before they get strung along and almost forced into performing or acting a way they really do not want to act.

Some passive people think they are not able to speak up or don't have the right to voice their opinion. Are they afraid of being liked or disliked, unloved or loved, and loosing out? The reactions to questions or suggestions that are posed by others often are allowed to lead us into the wrong decision that we don't want to be included in. Have you ever heard directive questions like: let's go do some drugs? Let's all go get drunk? Let's go make love? Let's go do something wild? Let's go do something dangerous? Let's go rob a bank? Let's skip school? Let's go to that old abandoned house down the street and . . .? The passive person just allows the event to take place by following passively along or agrees with the suggestion because . . . The answer is in the Why section of this book.

Impulsive behaviors and communication skills that were learned by the toddler and young child are continuing to be exhibited until the child goes back and fixes them to repair the psychosocial crisis.

If you want to have a more exciting and self- controlled type of life and are tired of following others for whatever the reason, continue to read this book, and try some of the suggestions that are included. The items suggested in this book will give you some positive insight and possibly an idea or two that can help you to live a more positive and progressive life. It may allow you to be the controller instead of the controlled.

As the dictionary defined being the object rather than the subject of action, so are you a mere object that is controlled and pushed around, the gofer, the fetcher, the one who waits for the leader to give direction and push you into continuing as an object? Or, a not with vitally or mentally active, unresponsive person? The most passive people tend to act as they are not mentally active. They are almost unresponsive. They are led into many situations that they haven't thought about as they are not mentally active and are unresponsive. They don't have the ability to respond on their own, and need the leader to order them to comply with their demands.

As you have grown and developed, you have most assuredly learned to have several styles of communication and methods to deliver your needs, wants and desires. Some of them may be the right way and some the wrong way or rather incorrect way of resolving issues in your life.

Chapter 8

LETS GET EVEN

Vindictive

The vindictive act seems to hurt the offender more than the originator of the problem. You can't get even with anyone, only yourself. Some use vindictive behaviors inwardly as they punish or hurt themselves to show the audience (parent, teacher, partner, etc.) that they will hurt and, you as the audience, respond with giving PITY or sympathy to the person, and that in itself fulfills their immediate need for attention.

I'll get even with you!!!! I'm going to . . . what?? How will you get even without costing yourself something greater?? It is almost impossible. *I'll run away from the situation and do something irrational.* What is the cost of that?? Well, running away will cost you your reputation or something greater. I'll *punch you in the face.* And now you get to face criminal charges and have a felony on your record for assault and battery. Are you going to use a weapon?? Then the consequences get greater. *I'll show you.* What great statements to set yourself up for additional costs and failures. And then!!! The person that you were going to show, hurt, hit, shoot, or whatever, wins and you loose. So what are you doing by threatening and attempting to hurt someone to get even or get back at?? You are only hurting yourself worse, and looking more irrational and immature. The only way to get back at someone is to show them by being more mature and rational, and proving your success.

Being appropriately assertive and not angry or vindictive is a very important skill for you to have in the Life Tool Box as it can make you Independent if you have the right tools or very Dependent if you do not have the right tools and skills to use. I have found that most people do not know how to appropriately communicate and, as a fact, most individuals learn to communicate from their parents, brothers, sisters, school teachers (but not a subject), pastor, friends, etc., and they use whatever they saw worked for someone else or themselves. You will continue to use those tools/skills until you find one that works better and is more successful. The facts are that usually people learn professional communications when they are working toward their Masters Degree and not before. Wow!!! There are about 3% of the population of the United States that have a

Masters Degree. Are you one of those? Probably not as 97% do not have one. Communication is something that everyone needs to know how to do while being assertive and appropriate so that they can achieve having their personal goals met and being more INDEPENDENT.

The next chapter will show different methods of Appropriate Assertive Communication Styles that you must practice over and over until you have mastered it and placed it in your Personal Tool Box.

Chapter 9

LEARNING HOW TO COMMUNICATE

Assertive, What Is It?

For someone to be assertive, they must learn to express themselves appropriately. Think before acting, use the proper phraseology when talking to others, and know what you really want for yourself. Stand on your own two feet when addressing situations, don't be passive aggressive and try to control the situation by anger. Use those thoughts of self-control and positive "I" statements. But first you have to know who you are and where you are headed. You have probably heard of "going off half-cocked", not thinking about all of the possible unwanted and undesired ramifications that may appear in the immediate future. Don't allow yourself to be controlled by others inappropriately and/or be pushed into things or situations that are not good for you. Take a stand; follow your thoughts to become more successful. Most often, to become successful in assertiveness, it will require many practice runs with role-play situations. This will help you understand how others will respond and how you will feel once you have stood up for what you think and feel is right for you.

Do you often find that others coerce you into thinking their way? Is it difficult for you to express your positive or negative feelings openly and honestly? Do you sometimes lose control and become angry with others who don't warrant it?

Answer to any of the above questions may be an expression of a common problem known as "lack of assertiveness."

What is Assertiveness?

Assertiveness is the ability to express yourself and your rights without violating the rights of others. The behavior or approach to the problem is appropriately direct, open, and honest communication, which is self-enhancing and expressive. Acting and being assertive will permit you to feel self-confident, and will generally gain you the respect of your peers and friends. Assertiveness can increase your chances for an honest relationship, and help you to feel better about yourself and your self-control in everyday situations. When you display assertiveness, it will, in turn, improve your decision-making ability and possibly your chances of getting what you really want from life.

Assertiveness primarily is a method of communication that allows you to express your thoughts and feelings to someone who clearly states what your needs are, and keeps the lines of communication open with those whom you are conferring. However, before you begin this wonderful method of assertiveness, you must make sure that you have a legitimate right to have those needs met, and keep in mind the following: the right to decide how to lead your life. This includes pursuing your own goals and dreams, and establishing your own priorities.

- The right to your own values, beliefs, opinions, and emotions, and the right to respect yourself for them, no matter the opinion of others.
- The right not to justify or explain your actions or feelings to others.
- The right to tell others how you wish to be treated.
- The right to express yourself and to say," I don't know," I don't understand," or even "I don't care." You have the right to take the time you need to formulate your ideas before expressing them.
- The right to ask for information or help without having negative feelings about your needs.
- The right to change your mind, to make mistakes, and to sometimes act illogically with full understanding and acceptance of the consequences.
- The right to like yourself even though you're not perfect, and to sometimes do less than you are capable of doing.
- The right to have positive, satisfying relationships within which you feel comfortable and free to express yourself honestly, and the right to change or end relationships if they don't meet your needs.
- The right to change, enhance, or develop your life in any way you determine.

You may react passively to events and circumstances when you do not believe that you possess these rights. You are likely to feel hurt, anxious and/or angry when you put the needs, opinions and judgments of others before your own. This type of passive or non-assertive behavior is often indirect, emotionally dishonest and, most of all, self-denying.

Many people feel selfish asserting their own rights and legitimate needs as they attend to others. For people to be considered selfish means that they have little or no regard for others and are only concerned with their own rights. Considering the other person's rights is a part of those rights that the assertive person considers as well.

Being assertive appropriately defuses others and helps us feel better after the appropriate delivery of communication.

First: Describe the thing that you like or dislike by using "I" statements, such as I really don't like feeling the way I do when I am let down by those things that just happened.

Second: Explain the circumstances of the disliked behavior: "I was let down and feel hurt because the house was nice and clean when I left and now the house is upside down".

Third: State your wishes: "I would like to return home and find the house in the same condition that I left it especially after I worked so hard to make it clean and neat like everyone in our house enjoys it being".

Fourth: Compromise when and if necessary. "Let's discuss what happened and see what I can do to help our home continue to be in the same condition when I get home as when I leave it".

Communication skills are learned throughout a lifetime and, as we grow older and realize that there are more times that we have arguments and fights and state things that we really don't mean just have an angry display of temper that hurts feelings and sometimes escalates to bizarre and nasty acts of Domestic Violence, then we oftentimes want to back up and unstate and undo the actions that we displayed in our behavior. Unfortunately, this 2-to-4-year-old behavior continues to repeat itself until a time when we learn new skills and how to have more self-control, and act like the adult or adolescent that we truly are.

Selfishness and Aggressiveness

When you behave in a destructive, aggressive manner, you are acting selfishly which places your emphasis on and violates the rights of others rather than being constructive and assertive.

Aggressiveness shows others that you are expressing your rights; however, these expressions are at the expense, degradation, or humiliation of another by being aggressive, being so forceful emotionally and/or physically that the rights of others are not allowed to be aired or considered. Most all acts of aggression usually result in others becoming angry or vengeful and, as such, it can work against your intentions and cause people to lose respect for you. You may feel an enormous ego boost and become self-righteous or superior at a particular time; however, after thinking things through, you may end up feeling guilty later.

What Assertiveness Will Not Do

Asserting yourself will not necessarily guarantee you happiness or fair treatment by others, nor will it solve all your personal problems or guarantee that others will be assertive and not aggressive. Just because you assert yourself does not mean you will always get what you want; however, lack of assertiveness is most certainly one of the reasons why conflicts occur in relationships. In many instances, you may have developed a pattern of being non-assertive with the other person in your relationship; then, when you take on the personal right of being assertive and voicing your desires without offending anyone, they become shocked that you have made a positive change that can lead to arguments and/or discussions. You must, therefore, with this desire to assert your rights, have a plan and techniques in your ToolBox that are clear and precise about what your rights are and how you want to express your desires without becoming aggressive.

Specific Techniques for Assertiveness

1. Be very specific and clear about what you want, think, and feel. The following statements will help you project this preciseness:

   - I want to..."
   - I don't want you to..."
   - Would you...?"
   - I liked it when you did that..."
   - I have a different opinion; I think that..."
   - I have mixed reactions. I agree with these aspects for these reasons..., but I am disturbed about these aspects for these reasons...

   You should express your desires to implement change in a positive manner to express your rights. This should be done by explaining what you do and don't mean, such as: "I don't want to break up over this, but I'd like to talk it through and see if we can prevent it from happening again."

2. Your approach should be direct. Tell your message to the person directly; you should not tell others and hope that it trickles back to that person who you want to have this information about your desires. Don't deliver your message to the group that that person just happens to be a member of or is associated with.

3. "Own" your personal message. Control your personal thoughts and messages from your own frame of reference and your conception of right versus wrong, good versus bad. You show others with ownership of personalized "I" statements such as "I don't agree with you" as compared to "You're wrong", or "I'd like you to mow the lawn" as compared to "You really should mow the lawn, you know". "You" statements put those people that you are communicating with on the defense, and will cause immediate argument or conflict. When you utilize those "you" statements, you are telling them that they are bad, wrong, and that they have to change for his or her own benefit when, in fact, it would please you. It will only foster resentment and resistance rather than understanding and cooperation.

4. Ask for feedback, "Am I being clear? How do you see this situation? What do you want to do?" Asking for feedback can encourage others to correct any misperceptions you may have as well as help others realize that you are expressing an opinion, feeling, or desire rather than a demand. Encourage others to be clear, direct, and specific in their feedback to you.

Learning to Become More Assertive

When you have decided to become more assertive, you should remember to use the skills that will help you the most, like using "I" when you want to accomplish something. It is a definite challenge for you to remember to use all of the skills, taking into consideration and remembering to pay close attention to your physical posture, giving eye contact in an appropriate manner; i.e., not rolling your eyes, using the correct tone of voice and hand gestures, and paying close attention to your own facial expressions. These skills are difficult to remember and use UNTIL you have them memorized and they become part of your inner you. These skills will require that you do some Role-Play. Some people will stand in front of a mirror and watch every move, every facial expression, hand gesture and body language that they are displaying. In addition to the role-play, you must have the tenacity to stick to it in every instance. Having the support of the people around you in your supportive relationships will help you and assist you in your journey to becoming more assertive and learning to apply all of your skills. The people that love and care about you will understand and will be your strongest assets to learning to be more assertive.

University of Illinois at Urbana-Champaign

Now that you are working on Communications while being appropriately assertive and not being Selfish and Aggressive in your talking techniques, these skills will enhance and help you grow in INDEPENDENCE while enhancing your self-esteem. We will look at some of the self-esteem issues in the next chapter and you will see how to apply many concepts.

Chapter 10

SELF-ESTEEM

What really is self-esteem?? Self-esteem is a part of all of humanity. It is comprised of our self-view and thoughts about us as individuals. How do you think of yourself when you look in the mirror?? Or when you don't look in the mirror but rather have a mental view within your mind of who you are? Do you consider yourself to be a respectable person? Self-esteem and self-view are all part of fitting in. It is a cultural view of ourselves. It is our self-reflection upon others. It is us thinking that we are the best that we can be, whatever that means to us. If you feel like junk, look like junk and dress like junk well, guess what?? You will be just that - junky to everyone who looks at you, hears you, and is close to you. Like the old story goes, if it looks like a duck, walks like a duck, it must be a duck. If we smell great, feel great, dress great and act great we must be great. Self-presentation requires much self-preparation, both mentally and physically. These things don't cost much either. In fact, I know a gentleman who dresses in clothes that are all designer items that he purchases from the Salvation Army and are still new with the tags on them when he purchases them. No one needs to know where you purchase the apparel that you own. Would it really matter that you purchased your Nike shirt at the Salvation Army for $4.00 instead of the store in the mall for $37.00 when both of them still have the tags on them?? Many retailers donate items to Goodwill and the Salvation Army for the tax benefits, and these are first-quality products with the tags or boxes that the item came with and some of them from the store that donated them. It does require the time to go to the stores and search the racks for just the right items. After all, the really great stuff is a prime target for the smart shoppers that are all around the store.

THE TRUE MEANING OF SELF-ESTEEM
by Robert Reasoner

MULES AND DONKEYS ARE ASSERTIVE AND SHOW POSITIVE SELF-ESTEEM, THEY KNOW WHAT THEY WANT, AND KNOW HOW THEY ARE, AND LIKE BEING THEMSELVES, THEY SAY THINGS LIKE "I WANT TO BE HERE, AND I CAN BE BECAUSE I AM A DONKEY".

Educators, parents, business and government leaders agree that, within our communities, we need to develop individuals with healthy or high self-esteem characterized by acceptance, tolerance and respect for others. These individuals who accept responsibility for their own actions show that they have integrity and take pride in their accomplishments. They display behaviors of being self-motivated, willing to take risks, capable of handling criticism in a loving and lovable manner. They seek the challenges and stimulation of worthwhile and demanding goals, and take command and control of their lives. In other words, we need to help promote the development of people who have authentic self-esteem because they trust their own being to be life-affirming, constructive, responsible and trustworthy.

Unfortunately, the term self-esteem is difficult to convey its genuine meaning as it is hampered by misconceptions and confusion about its true meaning. Some have referred to self-esteem as merely "feeling good" or having positive feelings about oneself. Others have gone so far as to equate self-esteem with egotism, arrogance, conceit, narcissism, a sense of superiority, a trait leading to violence. These characteristics should not be attributed to genuine and authentic self-esteem because they are actually defensive reactions to the lack of authentic self-esteem which is sometimes referred to as "pseudo self-esteem". Individuals that display behaviors conducive with low self-esteem are trying to prove themselves, be defensive or impress others with their importance. These individuals tend to use others for their own selfish gain. Some individuals act with arrogance and contempt towards others. They generally are deficient in having confidence in themselves, often have doubts about their worth and acceptability, and thus, are hesitant to take risks or expose themselves to failure. They most often blame others for their shortcomings and behaviors rather than take responsibility for their actions.

It has been documented many times that there is a positive correlation between low self-esteem and behaviors and such problems as violence, alcoholism, drug abuse, eating disorders, school dropouts, teenage pregnancy, suicide, and low academic achievement. In other words, those who display low self-esteem usually have many negative problems such as violence, alcoholism, drug abuse, eating disorders, school dropouts, teenage pregnancy, suicide, and low academic achievement. However, it is difficult to isolate low self-esteem as a primary cause using traditional experimental research methods, for low self-esteem is usually only one of several contributing factors that the individual is exposed to or utilizes as their individual self-destruct/protection method. What needs to be stressed is that self-esteem is a very critical component of any program that has the focus aimed at self-improvement or any rehabilitation program. Self-esteem is one of the few solutions that offer any of these individuals hope to correct these problems. Many prisons, self-improvement courses, counseling programs, and learning institutes, for example, have now introduced self-esteem programs to reduce recidivism and help those individuals not re-offend or relapse.

Since self-esteem is such a broad term and is utilized in many different manners by many different people in all walks of life, people, practitioners, attorneys, doctors, psychologists, counselors and the like have a difficult time narrowing down the brief overall meaning of the concept of self-esteem. This word has been examined from many different views as some look at it from the perspective of psychodynamic theory, developmental processes, cognitively, social cognitions, attitudes, experiential dimensions and some even use two or more facets. Since self-esteem has sociological and psychological dimensions, it is difficult to come up with a single comprehensive definition and keep both of those dimensions included.

There is, however, general agreement that the term self-esteem does include cognitive, affective, behavioral and spiritual elements. Cognitive elements are our thought processes; affective are our feelings within us; behavioral elements are how we display, or act out our thoughts and feelings; and, for those who have spiritual beliefs, also take into consideration the spiritual element of how we are viewed by God and how we act according to writings in scripture. When considering the cognitive aspect of self-esteem, this is what we think within our minds about ourselves, and how we compare ourselves to our world and the people in our daily lives. It is our perceived self or our realistic appraisal of how we truly see ourselves. The affective element refers to our feelings and emotions that we must take into consideration as our feelings affect the way that we behave. Our emotions are quite complicated and, to become more assertive and behave in appropriate manners, we must understand how we feel and learn how others consider how we feel when we use facial expressions and body language to show others about our emotions. Our behavioral element that is embedded in our self-esteem is most important to learn about and use in an appropriate manner. The aspects of behavior in our self-esteem are shown to others through our behavior of assertiveness, being decisive while being respectful of others, and our resilience to recover when traumatic or threatening things affect our thinking. The spirituality of our self-esteem is how knowledgeable we are about that spiritual being that we trust and believe in, what our scripture has taught us, and how others view our specific religious beliefs. Thus, self-esteem is difficult to define as it is multi-faceted just like the sides on a diamond have many different flat areas. However, self-esteem usually is stable and unchanging the majority of the time, but self-esteem can be changed if we choose to change our inner thinking processes.

Most importantly is that we should not loose self-esteem in attempting to find an accurate and simple definition. Nathaniel Branden, Ph.D., a well-known psychotherapist, defined self-esteem several years ago as "The disposition to experience oneself as being competent to cope with the basic challenges of life and of being worthy of happiness." Additionally, The National Association for Self-Esteem modified this to define self-esteem as "The experience of being capable of meeting life's challenges and being worthy of happiness." Christopher Murk, Ph.D., a psychology professor at Bowling Green University, reports in his book Self-Esteem: Research, Theory, and Practice that, of all the theories and definitions proposed, this description of self-esteem has best withstood the test of time in terms of accuracy and comprehensiveness.

Self-esteem is based on competence and worthiness, and the relationship of those two things that give us the meaning of how we live our lives. The worthiness component of self-esteem is often misunderstood and shown to believe that it is merely feeling good about ourselves. Actually, self-esteem is directly related to how we live up to the human values that we perceive ourselves as related to. It relates to how we help others grow and how we make commitments and live up to them, and that we have our inner personal feelings and thoughts about ourselves; that we believe we have integrity and self-satisfaction. It is our sense of competence about how well we make our decisions and follow through with those decisions in a positive and successful manner. Worthiness can be considered the sociological piece of self-esteem, and competence can be considered and thought of as our personal judgment of ourselves as it is related to our self-competence and self-worth that is based in reality.

The importance of this definition is for us to make the determination that we have authentic and healthy self-esteem versus pseudo or unhealthy self-esteem. It is our personal worth without being limited to our competence and worthiness. It is a strong sense of competence that will keep us from becoming arrogant, and help us focus on our personal values that are earned and not given. Our behaviors would be considered appropriate when we apply these concepts, or else we may fall into the low self-esteem behaviors of egotistic, egocentric, conceited, boasting or bragging, bullying, taking advantage of, or harming others. All are defensive tactics of **LOW SELF-ESTEEM.**

Some programs and strategies use methods and definitions that were not grounded in sound research, and they have added to the confusion of defining self-esteem. These programs showed that giving children unwarranted praise that was not based on accomplishment would help when in fact it hurt those children. These methods condoned the use of reciting boosters or mantras or affirmations that were made up and thought to be somewhat helpful to building authentic self-esteem which is most likely to result in an over-inflated sense of worth based on unrealistic self-concepts. It is valuable for one to strengthen one's sense of self-competence by using realistic and accurate self-appraisal, meaningful accomplishments, overcoming adversities, and bouncing back from failures.

It is not possible to have too much self-esteem; it is good for us to have high self-esteem. It is much like having good self-esteem just like being in good health, and it is almost impossible to be in too good of health
http://www.self-esteem-nase.org/

User Submitted Quotations.

- I'm good enough. I'm smart enough and, dog gone it, people like me.
- The dog is cool.
- How can you smell like a rose when you live in garbage.

- Stand tall for what you've earned, but not so tall that you overshadow what you have achieved.
- Happiness is a butterfly which, when pursued, is always beyond your grasp but, if you quietly sit down, it may land upon you.
- "I am such a beautiful person. How can I not love that person? I am so grateful for everything." - Clara and Yvon
- "The Mountain of Self-Esteem is built on the Isle of Competencies." - Samule C. Latterner, C.S.W.
- You will never get a hit if you don't get off the bench and bat.
- Those who can do,do; those who can't just talk about how good they could do it.
- Seek and ye shall find inner peace and spiritual satisfaction - look within.
- "God opposes the proud, but gives grace to the humble" ~God~
- The best way to improve your self-esteem is to understand yourself.
- Healthy self-esteem is a child's armor against the challenges of the world.
- "Everyday, and in every way, I am getting better and better." - Emile Coue (1857-1926)
- Monkey see, Monkey do!!!!!!!!!!!!
- Strive for what it is you want, and you will see there are no boundaries. Remember the squeaky wheel gets the grease!
- "My life has been one great big joke; a dance that's walked, a song that's spoke, I laugh so hard I almost choke when I think about myself." - Maya Angelou
- Embrace life with passion!
- To thine own self be true!
- There is nothing in the world that you can't do as a woman except stand up and pee and, as a man you can't give birth but it takes you to help create life.
- Self-esteem is a rating of how much you're hurting inside. Low self-esteem = pain.
- "The greatest evil that can befall man is that he should come to think ill of himself" - Goethe
- We are what we think we are.

- "Whatever the mind can conceive and believe, the mind can achieve." - Dr. Napoleon Hill
- "If you think you can or you think you can't, you're right" - Henry Ford
- No matter what you are, always accepted by one - God - So accept yourself, and just say that this is the way I am, if no one can accept me, at least God can. And, in the long life, that's all that matters.
- You can't be a smart cookie with a crummy attitude!!!
- If someone calls you something and you know that you are not one . . .
- The price you put on yourself is paid for you.
- Follow the crowd, and soon you will be lost in it.
- You have never seen a hearse towing a U-haul trailer! This life is not a dress rehearsal.
- If you don't paddle your own canoe, you don't move.
- Believe in yourself!
- Trust yourself.
- Show your true self! Don't be shy!
- You won't gain respect from others if you don't respect yourself.
- "If you want something you've never had before, you've got to do something you've never done before." - Drina Reed
- "Reach high, for stars lie hidden in your soul. Dream deep, for every dream precedes the goal." - Pamela Vault Star
- I am what I am, and that's all that I am no more, no less, just the way I like it.
- If you believe in yourself, no one else can hurt you, for you are your own rainbow!!
- "If God wanted me otherwise, He would of made me otherwise." - Goethe
- "Celebrate the gifts in you by achieving them." - Bridgette smith.
- "There is no way to happiness. Happiness is the way." - The Buddha
- Have faith in yourself and others will have faith in you.
- If God wanted me Otherwise, He would of made me Otherwise --Goethe
- SELF-ESTEEM - What is it? Who got it? Do I need it? How

do I get some? When I got sober, to me it did seem I needed to get that self-esteem. I asked some 'old timers' – Would it keep me off of that dead-end street? They said, yes but there's someone I had to meet; not just meet but really get to know, down to the depths of their very soul, I said, where is this person, what should I do? They said, look inside to find that which is you, the one that once was but now has been lost, you must find him again no matter the cost. When you do, you must start to work, so you can become a man instead of a jerk. I'm listnin', I'm thinkin', I know what you mean, but must you do this to get self-esteem? They said, not only will it keep you alive, but we know that without it you'll never thrive. I said, Ego and self-esteem - aren't they the same, the only difference being the name? They said, an inflated ego is really a sham, to hide the fears of the real man. Self-esteem, like respect, takes time to grow, like a good roast, well basted, cooked slow. I said, what about crossing that line to conceit, where you think you are better than all you meet? They said, you don't need to worry, not one bit, your friends will tell you when you're full of it. So, we hope you now know that in your recovery, the outcome hinges on self-discovery. When you know and admit who you really be, only then will you start to set yourself free. You can then become a man that you'd respect, one that almost died because of neglect. Over time as I worked very hard on recovery, I made an astounding, amazing discovery. The harder I worked on who I could be, the more I was happy, joyous and free. by T.O.M. (4/2/02)

- SELF - WHERE MYSELF IS CONCERNED I MUST GRACIOUSLY RECUSE MYSELF FROM THIS MATTER. by T.O.M. (May, 2002)
- I will praise thee, for I am fearfully and wonderfully made: marvelous are thy works... -Psalm 139:14
- Links are what make us stronger and more knowledgeable! Find your support group (your friends, family, teachers, and leaders) to help you be strong!
- Let your voice shine, and help others be heard.
- No matter what you say or do, to me I STILL am a worthwhile person.

- The Great Reality can only be found within; why don't we go there more often?
- True self-esteem comes from God's gifts to us; redemption from sin, love through his grace and everlasting life...What more is there in life except salvation from ourselves? Love unconditionally, and our soul united with God?
- Self-esteem is found in God and God alone!

Feeling positive about yourself and showing the people that you come into contact with that you are a Positive Person who can become more INDEPENDENT and has good or a higher self-esteem has a very positive good feeling about it, and now you should be working on all of the positive attributes, skills and tools. You do have to practice and practice as it takes effort to be successful at anything. Those feelings that are positive will help you in the next chapter as you grow in INDEPENDENCE and figure out where you fit in the community and your world.

Chapter 11
LEARNING HOW TO FIT

Fitting In

What does fitting in with the rest of the group mean? The definition of fitting in can mean a variety of things from wearing the same type clothing, having the same hairstyle, talking with the same type accent, thinking some of the same thoughts, and being the same age as the majority of the group. To fit or not to fit? The times when we attempt to join a specific group of people and the fit just isn't the right one, we feel and think that it is uncomfortable, and it causes some stress to us. This stress may cause us to find another group to try to fit into or make personal changes to try to fit into the one that we are currently hanging out with. This group formation and finding the correct group is a very difficult task for some, especially for those who think that they have some unique quality that no one else would understand or be able to relate to. When standing out in the crowd and making a fashion statement, being totally different and having everyone look at you and know that you are different requires leadership, and that person must be willing to defend that position. This doesn't mean that you have to become a world heavy weight boxer to defend your title either. What it does mean is that you should be able to become assertive and lead your ideas and thinking in an appropriate manner. Assertiveness is a type of aggressiveness without violence. It is having the ability to stand up for what you think and what you want, desire, and love.

Now that you have worked diligently toward all of those skills and are beginning to fit better as your feelings of self-pride are building, you can see how aggression and anger are really good attributes to have, and how to appropriately use anger for your good and not have it interfere with your life by allowing others to push your buttons.

Chapter 12

AGGRESSIVE, WHAT IS IT?
Expressing your anger

To express your anger in a way that is appropriate and legal is or should be a most important thing for anyone in today's society to do. Remember, anger is a natural form of emotion that everyone experiences both emotionally and physiologically. When we start to become angry, our endocrine system of hormones kicks in and starts to rig our bodies with all of the necessary chemicals that we need to protect ourselves. This chemical rush in our bodies is to aid us in FLIGHT OR FIGHT so we can be successful in our battle and SURVIVE. The key here is to maintain THINKING. Don't let your mind shut down and forget about rules, laws, acceptance and control of yourself. Try to remember that there are numerous methods to control yourself and express your anger that will lead you to more successful anger expression. To control or be controlled, that is the question.

The natural way to express your anger is in the pre-historic and caveman method of becoming aggressive. Anger is a natural and adaptive way to respond to threats. You had the ability to express your anger at birth, with little or no control of yourself. I hope that you have mentally grown since the time of your birth, and can control yourself a little more now!!!

Let's brainstorm a little about how you could resolve your anger. You could lash out physically and destructively at anyone that angered you; you could throw dishes, break windows, shoot people, yell and scream, drive really fast and dangerously, storm out, hit the person or persons, bash people with objects, etc., acting much like your cave-man/woman self.

Recognizing Anger

We know when we are very mad, but anger and aggression come in many forms, some quite subtle. Look inside yourself for more anger. This list (Maslow, 1972) of behaviors and verbal comments said to others or only thought to ourselves may help you uncover some resentments you were not aware of:

<u>Direct behavioral signs</u>:

1. Assaultive: physical and verbal cruelty, rage, slapping, shoving, kicking, hitting, threaten with a knife or gun, etc.
2. Aggression: overly critical, fault- finding, name-calling, accusing someone of having immoral or despicable traits or motives, nagging, whining, sarcasm, prejudice, flashes of temper.
3. Hurtful: malicious gossip, stealing, trouble-making.
4. Rebellious: anti-social behavior, open defiance, refusal to talk.

<u>Direct verbal or cognitive signs</u>:

1. Open hatred and insults: "I hate your guts." "I'm really mad." "You're so damn stupid."
2. Contempt and disgust: "You're a selfish SOB." "You are a spineless wimp, you'll never amount to anything."
3. Critical: "If you really cared about me, you'd..." "You can't trust _____."
4. Suspicious: "You haven't been fair." "You cheated!"
5. Blaming: "They have been trying to cause me trouble."
6. I don't get the respect I deserve: "They just don't respect the owner (or boss or teacher or doctor) any more."
7. Revengeful: "I wish I could really hurt him."
8. Name-calling: "Guys are jerks." "Women are bitches." "Politicians are self-serving liars."
9. Less intense but clear: "Well, I'm a little annoyed." "I'm fed up with..." "I've had it!" "You're a pain." "I don't want to be around you."

Thinly veiled behavioral signs:

1. Distrustful, skeptical.
2. Argumentative, irritable, indirectly challenging.
3. Resentful, jealous, envious.
4. Disruptive, uncooperative, or distracting actions.
5. Unforgiving or unsympathetic attitude.
6. Sulky, sullen, pouting.
7. Passively resistant, interferes with progress.
8. Given to sarcasm, cynical humor, and teasing.
9. Judgmental; has a superior or holier-than-thou attitude.

Thinly veiled verbal signs:

1. "No, I'm not mad, I'm just disappointed, annoyed, disgusted, put out, or irritated."
2. "You don't know what you are talking about." "Don't make me laugh."
3. "Don't push me, I'll do it when I get good and ready."
4. "Well, they aren't my kind of people."
5. "Would you buy a used car from him?"
6. "You could improve on..."
7. "Unlike social work, my major admits only the best students."

Indirect behavioral signs:

1. Withdrawal: quiet remoteness, silence, and little communication especially about feelings.
2. Psychosomatic disorders: tiredness, anxiety, high blood pressure, and heart disease. Actually, college students with high hostility scores had, 20 years later, become more overweight with higher cholesterol and hypertension, had drunk more coffee and alcohol, had smoked more cigarettes, and generally had poorer health (Friedman, 1991).
3. Depression and guilt.
4. Serious mental illness: paranoid schizophrenia.
5. Accident-proneness and self-defeating or addictive behavior, such as drinking, over-eating, or drugs.
6. Vigorous, distracting activity (exercising or cleaning).

7. Excessively submissive, deferring behavior.
8. Crying.

Indirect verbal signs:

1. "I just don't want to talk."
2. "I'm disappointed in our relationship."
3. "I feel bad all the time."
4. "If you had just lost some weight."
5. "I'm really swamped with work, can't we do something about it?"
6. "Why does this always happen to me?"
7. "No, I'm not angry about anything - I just cry all the time."

How angry are you?

There are many, many, many frustrations in our daily lives; one could easily become constantly irritated. The Zen Buddhists said over 3,000 years ago that Life is a hassle. Perhaps more important than the variety of things that anger us, is (1) the intensity or severity of our anger and (2) how much control we have over our anger. That is, how close are we to losing control and going into a NO-THINKING ZONE. Most of the people that have attended my groups think and feel the need to gain more control over their anger.

How much of a temper do you have? Ask yourself these kinds of questions:

- Do you have a quick or a hot temper? Do you suppress or hide your anger (passive-aggressive or victim)?
- Do you get irritated when someone gets in your way? Fails to give you credit for your work? Criticizes your looks or opinions or work? Gives themselves advantages over you?
- Do you get angry at yourself when you make a foolish mistake? Do poorly in front of others? Put off important things? Do something against your morals or better judgment?
- Do you drink alcohol or use drugs? Do you get angry or mellow when you are high? Research clearly shows that alcohol

and drugs are linked with aggression. Drinking decreases our judgment and increases our impulsiveness, so watch out.

You probably know all about your temper and how angry and NOT THINKING you become. But check your opinion against the opinion of you held by relatives and friends.

There also are several tests that measure anger, e.g. Spielberger (1988).

A case of jealous anger

Bill and Jane had gone together a long time, long enough to wear off the thrill and take each other for granted. The place where this was most apparent was at dances and parties. Bill was very outgoing. He liked to "circulate" and meet people, so he would leave Jane with a couple of her friends, and he would go visit all his old buddies. This bothered Jane; she would have liked to go along. But what really bothered Jane was Bill's eye for beautiful women. As he moved around greeting his friends, he looked for the best-looking, relatively unattached woman there. Bill was nice looking, a good dancer, and not at all shy. He'd introduce himself, find out about the woman, tell some funny stories about what he had done and, if it were a dance, ask her to dance. Eventually, he would excuse himself and come back over to Jane and her friends. He just enjoyed meeting new people and dancing at parties.

Jane resented this routine. She had told Bill how she felt many times. He told her that she was being ridiculous. Jane felt much more anger, hurt, jealousy, and distrust inside than she let show. She was usually quiet and "cool" for a little while but pretty soon she would dance with Bill and it seemed like she got over it. Yet, even the next day, she would think about what had happened and cry. Around lunch time, she would wonder what Bill was doing. A little fantasy would flash through her mind about Bill calling up the woman he danced with and asking her out to lunch. That would hurt her, too.

Now let's look at understanding your anger, and how some inappropriate situations come up and how to handle them.

Chapter 13

UNDERSTANDING ANGER

The nature of the person.

Konrad Lorenz (1966) believed that species, both animal and human, survived by having an aggressive instinct, that protected their territory and young, and insured only the strongest individuals survived. Freud believed in a death of aggressive instinct because he saw so much violence, sadism, war, and suicide. The sociobiologists, noting the frequency that we go to war, also suggest that we have inherited an aggressive nature, a tendency to dominate and control so we lash out at anything that gets in our way.

Research shows us that stimulation of certain parts of animals' brains leads to aggression. Stimulation of other parts stops aggression. We don't understand very much about how this works. In 1966, Charles Whitman killed his wife and mother because "I do not consider this world worth living in...", then climbed a tower on the University of Texas campus and fired his rifle at 38 people. He killed 14 before being killed. An autopsy revealed a large tumor in the limbic system of his brain (where the aggression "centers" are in animal brains). In epileptic patients with implanted electrodes, in rare cases, violence follows stimulation of certain parts. Abnormal EEG's have been found among repeat offenders and aggressive people. So, aggression may sometimes have a physical basis. Brain damage can be caused in many ways (Derlega and Janda, 1981).

Chemistry of our Aggression

Aggression may also have a chemical, hormonal, or genetic basis, too. A large survey of adopted children has found that living with an adoptive parent who committed crimes is less risky than merely having the genes from a person who committed crimes (Mednick, Gabrielli & Hutchings, 1984). The human gene is very powerful but, obviously in animals, certain breeds of dogs, like pit bulls, are more vicious than others. More aggressive breeds can be developed, e.g., roosters, rats or fighting bulls. Maybe we should work on genetics to develop kinder, gentler, smarter humans.

Other physiological factors regarding aggression seem to be involved. Examples: high testosterone (male sex hormone) is associated with more unfaithfulness, more sex, more divorce, more competitiveness, and anti-social behavior. It is also known that a viral infection like rabies causes violent behavior. About 90% of women report being irritable before menstruation. Furthermore, 50% of all crimes by women in prison occurred during their menstrual period or premenstrual period. By chance, only 29% of crimes would have occurred during those eight days. Hypoglycemia (low blood sugar) increases during the premenstrual period, and it causes irritability. About 3 times in 1,000, a male inherits an extra X or Y chromosome, so they are XYY or XXY, instead of XY. At one time it was thought that XYY and XXY males committed more violent crimes. Now it appears that this isn't true, but these males are arrested earlier and more often. So we can't forget about our inheritance. There is so much we need to learn,including all of thesepossibilities: instinct, heredity, hormones, or brain dysfunction - the aggression occurs without apparent provocation from the environment (although there is almost always a "target"). According to some of these theories, the need or desire to be aggressive is boiling within each of us and seeks opportunities to express itself. This anger and aggression is permitted to escape the moment that we stop thinking and enter the NO THINKING ZONE. There is also clear evidence that alcohol consumption and hotter temperatures help to release aggression, but no one thinks there is something in alcohol or heat that generates meanness, anger and aggression. The socialization process that we go through in life, i.e., becoming a mature person, involves taming these destructive, savage, egocentric self-serving urges that probably helped us humans survive during the caveman era of one million years ago but threatens our survival today.

It is obvious from these "signs of anger" that anger is frequently a concealed or disguised emotion. And, why not? Getting mad is scary... and potentially dangerous especially when we enter the NO THINKING ZONE. One common way that people often behave, is that of expressing suppressed anger, has been given a special name: **passive-aggressiveness**. It is releasing your anger by being passive or subtly oppositional. For example, such a person may be "tired," unresponsive, act like he/she "doesn't understand," be late frequently, exaggerate others' faults, pretend to agree ("sure, whatever"), be tearful, be argumentative, be forgetful, deny anger ("nothing's wrong"), procrastinate, and frequently be clumsy or sick (Hankins, 1993). Many of these traits and behaviors are listed above.

There is another related form of concealed anger: feeling like a victim. Feeling victimized assumes that someone or some situation has mistreated you. But a person who specializes in constantly feeling like a victim may not identify or accuse his/her abuser. Instead, he/she generally feels that the world is against him/her, that others vaguely intend to make him/her miserable. Victims usually feel helpless; therefore, they take little responsibility for what has happened to them. They think they were terribly mistreated in the past, but they now seem unable to accept love and support, e.g., if you offer them help, they never get enough, or if you try to cheer them up, it seldom works. A victim is much more likely to sulk, pout, look unhappy, or lay a guilt trip on someone than to get angry. They play games: "Why does it always happen to me?" or "Yes, but" (no one's ideas or suggestions will do any good). The self-pitying, pessimistic, sad, jealous victim is surely sitting on a mass of hostility.

Both the passive-aggressive and the victim are likely to be aware of their anger even though it is largely denied by game playing and "You're not OK", or put down games without being aware of his/her anger. Anger expresses itself in many forms: cynic, nay-sayer, critic, bigot, etc. Potter-Efron & Potter-Efron (1995) Describe ten different styles of expressing anger; this may help you identify your type and help you stop it.

Eventually you will get into a personal romantic relationship or at least have a close friend. The need to resolve issues and have a lasting relationship is a task that takes a lot of practice.

Most individuals learned this from other people that were not successful, and attempt to figure out what might work or not work from those unsuccessful tools and skills. Some people look back to their early childhood; possibly Uncle Bob would use anger and aggression toward his loved ones and win his battle. And you as a child said to yourself "I don't want to use Uncle Bob's methods" and "I'll pick to use the nextdoor neighbor's methods". Those methods did not work well either. In the next chapter we will look at marital conflicts and those positive skills that can be applied in several circumstances as you develop and become more INDEPENDENT.

Chapter 14

MARITAL CONFLICT

Most of the traditional marriage vows are emotionally moving and express a noble commitment: "I take thee, for better or for worse... until death do us part." However, we often come to dislike many things about our partner, leading to very serious conflicts. Indeed, although all start with sincere intentions, today almost 50% of all marriages end in divorce in spite of enormous pressures to stay married. Why do we have the pressures? If marriage is considered a sacred public pledge or even "a union made in heaven," then divorce might be regarded as a sin (like in the Catholic and other churches) or, at least, a violation of a solemn promise or a legal contract. In addition to external pressures from family and divorce courts, there are also intense personal needs to "make it work" because it seems as though "you have failed" if your marriage fails.

Many marriages fail but do not end in divorce - the so-called "empty shell" marriage. These marriages may not have intense conflicts; indeed, they may be void of feelings. There must be disappointment in such marriages, however.

Most married people initially try to build a smooth, close, safe relationship, preferably one without friction. During this process, sometimes the roles for husband and wife become very rigidly defined; there is no freedom, no room for growth or change. Sometimes people think they need to pretend to be or feel some way to appeal to their spouse; there is little honesty and intimacy if you think your spouse may not **accept** you as you really are, i.e., for better or for worse. Acceptance of those little irritating things that go on within our lives as partners is a very important area of concern.

Fullerton (1977), in the mid-70's, explained how "the perfect wife" becomes sad and angry. Some women with self-doubts may be unusually anxious to please her new husband. She tries to do everything the way he would want it done. She thinks of all of his needs and puts them before her's or the children's. She believes: "If I'm the good, perfect wife, I will be loved." Eventually, being perfect with housecleaning, children and diapers, being a subservient and obedient woman becomes more and more tiresome and boring. She becomes resentful, upset and angry. And then, some evening when her husband arrives home from working late and finds her still moping the floor, he asks, "Are you *still* cleaning?" She bursts into tears. She cries because it is either go into a rage against her husband (which she - the perfect wife - can't do), or turn her anger inward on herself. She increases the self-criticism, clings more desperately to the husband, and feels more and more like crying, becoming more and more depressed with her situation.

The 1970's "perfect wife" was also prone to be jealous. According to Fullerton, a female was likely to get her sense of worth from a male - her father, her boyfriend, her husband and, later, her sons. She may have gone from being Daddy's little girl to being someone's wife without ever becoming a person and really knowing herself first. She was dependent on her looks and on being a "good girl" and "perfect wife" in order to be loved. She saw her husband as having strength and purpose; he was her whole life. Even when he was at work, she carried on an inner dialogue with him. She made her decisions in terms of what he would want and expect. Being so needy and unsure of her self-worth, naturally she would be jealous of anything that took his time - his work, his friends, his interests, etc. She was too insecure and too "perfect" to confront him, but eventually the jealousy may burst through, especially if she imagined another woman is involved. Once a jealous rage has occurred, it tends to reoccur. If he were innocent, it would be hard to prove. If she found out there is another woman, she was crushed. She felt betrayed, lost, scared, worthless, and angry. She might decide all men are no good, or she might look for another one who desires her. Women are changing and evolving but any woman over 40 can remember those times.

Husbands may also become angry, threatened, and jealous, too. An insecure male may, just like the wife, become dependent on his wife's adoration. She makes him feel good about himself. He may want her to "stay home" (too many men out there in the work place). He is jealous of anyone or anything that gets her attention. Tragically, that sometimes includes their own first-born child. The man may be ashamed to admit feeling resentful of his own child. Yet, he feels left out and betrayed; the wife is bewildered and unable to relieve his pain because the problem is inside him - his self-doubt (Fullerton, 1977). Men still want to be in control; they haven't changed as much as women have since the 1970's which stems from the days of the caveman. This causes more problems -girls/women are becoming more independent, boys/men are remaining dependent, tough, macho, and violent. Our culture is still inclined to say, "boys will be boys," but male possessiveness, dominance, and violence must be condemned and changed. Hopefully, men will eventually evolve and understand and accept the woman of the future instead of living in the caveman era.

In some families, the marital conflict is denied but gets expressed against another family member, often the oldest or the second child. That family member becomes the whipping boy or the scapegoat of the family. This displaced hostility is very harmful to the child because there is no way to escape (since the child has no control over the real source of the anger). The child may be accused of bad traits that the parent has (called projection) or of bad traits one parent resents in the other partner. For example, if the wife feels the husband is a liar and a cheat, she may accuse the son of these traits, and ask her husband to punish the son (indirectly letting the husband know how much she resents those traits). The husband's shame may get turned into self-righteous wrath with the son which eventually can cause great harm to the child. The parental expectations of the son to be dishonest may also become a self-fulfilling prophecy, whereby the son will say to himself "if they never believe me anyhow, I might as well lie."

No one believes that their marriage will be like this but, in fact, the problems of the two-career marriages without children would be very different. Those types of marriages may be financially better; however, the dual- career family has their own problems that are mostly quite unique.

Dealing with the "enemy of lovers"

Like scapegoating, many marital arguments or lovers' quarrels conceal the real conflict. Arguments over money may really be about who has the most power or about not getting enough attention or recognition. This kind of "fighting" can confront us with the truth, stripping away phoniness and deception, and giving us a chance to deal with the real problems realistically. (It may also encourage nasty criticism and the expression of raw emotions that damage the relationship, depending on the personalities involved. Especially when you enter the NO THINKING ZONE. The pros and cons of "fair fighting" are considered.)

All close relationships experience some friction. No thinking person will always agree with us. The thrill of being with your new lover wears off after some time. Certain wishes and dreams about marriage will not ever come true. Partners at times want things from us that we can't or won't give. Criticism and resentment tend to be expressed in irritating ways and sometimes very nasty ways. So many human personality factors annoy us; we tell ourselves that people and things should be different. It is frustrating when we can't understand why someone would do the things that they do. What was "cute" when dating may become very irritating, e.g., a partner's loudness or bossiness or indecisiveness. Some partners have said that their partner squeezes the toothpaste tube in the middle and "that just drives me nuts. It is all I can think about is fixing that tube". Or the tissue roll is placed on the holder with the leading edge facing out/in and "that really bugs me". Even good traits, like being understanding or rational or in control of your temper, can be infuriating to a partner who is ashamed of his/her emotionality. A partner may **accept** one of your traits, say shyness, and until he/she meets a good-looking, outgoing person, then he/she may suddenly resent it.

Maslow (1971) had a "Grumble Theory" that says: "The grass looks greener on the other side of the fence *and* dead on our side." He felt life was a series of ups and downs; accomplishments and relationships only give us a temporary high, and soon we are taking our lover/partner for granted and then grumbling again. Marriage is an example of this viewpoint: John and Jane were in love, they got married, had two beautiful children and were to be blissfully happy but, after several years, they take each other for granted - their grass looks brown and uninteresting. So, John begins thinking that he is missing out, and starts looking at other women and eventually is attracted to another woman who tells him how talented and interesting he is. Jane is also attracted to successful, attentive males and to a challenging, exciting career. The risk is that John and/or Jane will turn the unexciting and boring lifestyle "taken for granted" feelings into active dislike or disdain. "I can't stand Jane" or "I hate being at home." Maslow observed that high-level self-actualizers focused on getting on with living according to their values and avoided blaming and resenting others or discounting the past. Few of us are self-actualizers, however.

When hostility builds up inside, it eventually gets released - sometimes on the wrong person or issue. Often the tirade is a repetitious emotional harangue, obviously venting the anger rather than communicating. It may include vicious, nasty, cutting, insulting, offensive accusations. Both people are likely to become hostile and start playing "hard ball", and becoming vindictive and won't give in, not even a little bit. In addition to the release of the poison that may be hard to forgive, the fighters are usually trying, albeit ineffectively, to change each other into the new type person that they want for that moment. This often takes place around the 3rd year of the relationship, not the 7-year itch as some have stated. This greener-grass thinking is how our ancestors, the cave people, progressed thousands of years ago. They would hit the wonderful woman on the head, drag her to the cave, have babies and leave in about 3 years when the baby was old enough to care a little for themselves. The man would then go off to expand his gene pool. Have you ever noticed how hard we work to change others, and how little we work on changing ourselves or our expectations of others?

Trying to get our way

There are two tactics that are usually used for us to get our own way: (1) reasoned arguments, and (2) manipulation via bargaining, hinting, and use of emotions, deceit, or coercion. According to Johnson and Goodchilds (1976), 45% of women use emotions (usually sadness) and 27% of men do (usually anger). Four times as many women as men use helplessness as an appeal. You lose self-respect and the respect of others when you use weakness to manipulate others, however. Three times as many men as women use knowledge and present facts as a basis for winning an argument. Androgynous women are more like men. Unfortunately, the woman who takes a direct, rational, factual approach is considered "pushy", while a similar male is seen as competent. Fortunately, this is changing as both men and women evolve from the caveperson days and start to think. I think that you will be less likely to fall into the psychological pitfalls of using manipulation and other coercive methods if you know they exist.

Anger is nothing more than an attempt to make someone feel guilty - **Jampolsky,** 1985.

Finding better ways to resolve anger in relationships

Lerner (1985) considers anger to be a signal that something is wrong in a relationship. Often, we are angry because we are feeling put down, neglected, dealt with unfairly, infantilized, insulted, or cheated in some way. Therefore, the real problem is *not* the anger, but rather the task is to right whatever is wrong in the relationship. This is Lerner's main theme. She points out that the usual ways of handling irritating circumstances in a relationship - either being "nice" or being "hateful" - do not ordinarily change the situation. For example, the suppression of negative feelings (being "nice") usually means being weak, passive, and compliant which stores up more and more anger and eventually results in an ineffective hateful "explosion" or in "emotional distancing." On the other hand, the 1960's notion of "letting it all hang out" (and venting your anger) whenever you feel like it, is not only ineffective but has its hazards too: low self-esteem, feeling unable to relate, and guilt. Thus, neither the nasty attacks and hateful bitching of unfair fights, as we've seen, nor the uncommunicative empty-shell marriages are capable of solving the underlying marital problems. They only make things worse. What will help?

Lerner lists four useful approaches:

1.   Finding out what is really bugging you (your needs, frustrations, regretted choices, blocked dreams, etc.),
2.   learning to use new, better communication skills, such as "I" statements,
3.   gaining insight into your "dance of anger" and adopting new "steps" out of the old routine, and
4.   recognizing both parties' efforts to maintain the status quo of destructive fighting or passive withdrawal rather than maturely resolving the underlying problems.
5.   Resistance is a common barrier to changing the anger "dance." When desirable changes are initiated by one person in a relationship, Murry Bowen, a family therapist, says the partner frequently opposes the changes. For example, if the wife decides to develop her own social life rather than beg and

badger her reluctant husband to go out more, the husband's opposition to change often takes these forms:

1. "What you are doing (or about to do) is wrong."
2. "Stop being this way, and it will be okay."
3. "If you don't change back, some serious things will happen."

It takes courage to stand up to these challenges and threats, and proceed with improving your life, rather than keep on dancing the anger waltz.

There are various dances of anger. There may be disagreements - how much to socialize, spend, see relatives, watch TV, have sex, etc. - and anger flares, but nothing changes. One may seek more attention and love, while the other is emotionally unresponsive; both may get irritated, but nothing changes. One partner is over-involved with the children; the other is under-involved, and both complain, but nothing changes. One partner tries to change the other person but can't. Actually, the frustrated partner could change his/her own behavior and meet his/her own needs in other ways, but too often this independent action is not seriously considered and/or the partner strongly resists such changes. To meet your own needs requires a clear sense of purpose, confidence, independence, and persistence.

This willingness to be our own person and to move in our own direction, alone if necessary, is important but very scary (even in this age of sexual equality). It stops us from clearly expressing our basic disappointments in a relationship so the troubles never get resolved. Also, we are often afraid of unleashing our own anger, as well we should be, but the fear frequently inhibits our clear thinking about alternative ways of resolving the problems, including tactfully asserting our rights and preferences in that situation. The anger and these fears (of separation and destruction) also interfere with our exploring the sources and background of our own anger. This lack of self-understanding also reduces the keenness and flexibility of our problem- solving ability. Some quiet contemplation of our history, our situation, and our true emotions might help.

Triangles often play a role, without our awareness, in the creation of conflict and anger with a person. That is, we suppress anger towards one person (a boss or a spouse) and displace it to a scapegoat (a supervisee or a child). The scapegoat often never suspects that the anger is generated by someone else; he/she just feels disliked and persecuted. This arrangement permits us to use displacement to avoid facing and working on our own inter-personal difficulties. Whenever anger becomes a chronic condition, an unending dance, ask: Where might all this emotion come from? Is it a "left-over" from your original family? Is this displaced anger yielding a payoff to someone, e.g., do you and your spouse get to work on a "problem child" together? Is over-involvement between two people (say, father and daughter) a cause for mom and dad to fight? What would happen if the third party avoided forming a triangle and stayed out of any conflict between the other two people, e.g., if mom let father and son resolve their own fights? Does constantly worrying and working on relationship problems (your's or someone else's) divert your attention away from running your own life wisely?

The major unhealthy roles we tend to act out under stress and when angry are

a. the blamer, critic, or hot head,
b. the withdrawn, independent, or emotionally unreachable person,
c. the needy, "let's talk," or overly demanding partner,
d. the incompetent, "sick," or disorganized one, and
e. the know-it-all "I have no problems; I'll handle yours" rescuer. Do you recognize yourself and the people you have conflicts with? Try to avoid these roles. Start to change in small, carefully planned ways using good assertiveness. Also, avoid talking to anyone (beyond a brief factual consultation - no gossiping) about a third person who is upsetting you; if your underlying purpose is really to recruit support for your side, it may set up a triangle which is unhealthy. Deal directly with the person who is bothering you; keep others out of it (unless you seek therapy). Of course, older children or relatives can be told that you are having marital problems, if that is needed, but don't ask them to take sides.

Two more recent publications can help you understand anger and marital fights (Wile, 1993; Maslin, 1994). Both books suggest ways to resolve the cognitive origins of anger and re-establish love in the marriage.

Dr. E. Thomas Carroll II, M.A. LMHC

A long-term concern; an important problem

We have seen that anger is common but dreadfully destructive in human relations. Most of us dislike certain kinds of people, maybe "prejudiced, redneck clods," maybe "rude, demanding, lazy people on welfare," maybe "critical, arrogant bosses or teachers." If we are lucky, we can avoid conflict situations. However, if all of us would learn to control our irritation, jealousy, resentment, violence, prejudice, psychological putdowns, etc., wouldn't it be a much better world? Of course it would, but such goals seem so idealistic to many people; they think it is nonsense. People say "you can't change human nature." These defeatist attitudes prolong human misery. I don't think it is impossible (in a couple of generations) to get people to tolerate, even to love each other. It is an enormous task but such a worthy one that we must not give up. Instead, we must dedicate ourselves to improving the world, starting with ourselves.

The pessimist, who believes there will always be hatred and war, should note that the most primitive people on earth (discovered in the Philippines in 1966) are gentle and loving. They have no word for war. How do they control their aggression? What is their system? The entire tribe discourages mean, inconsiderate behavior, and encourages cooperation from an early age. Everyone is expected to provide a good, loving model for the children (Nagler, 1982). Please note: This non-aggressive culture was developed without modern education, without great scholars, research and books, without powerful governments working for peace, and without any of the world's great religions. If that primitive tribe can learn to love, why can't we? It may not be too difficult after all. Nagler makes an impassioned plea for non-violence in our time.

The other bit of history I want to share with you is from Seneca, a Roman philosopher-educator, who served several emperors until Nero executed him in 65 AD at age 61. He was an extraordinary person. Seneca wrote a book, *De Ira* (Of Anger), which has been summarized by Hans Toch (1983). In it, Seneca proposed theories about aggression and self-help methods remarkably similar to the best we have today. It is humbling, but it suggests that common anger problems may not be that hard to solve (we have been too busy waging war for the last 2,000 years to work on reducing violence). Seneca said "hostile aggression" is to avenge an emotional injury. "Sadistic aggression," with practice, becomes habitual by frightening others and, in that way, reduces self-doubts (negative reinforcement). He noted that anger is often an overkill because we attribute evil to the other person or because the other person has hit our psychological weak spot, lowering our self-esteem. Sounds just like current theories, right?

There are some subjects about which you will learn the truth more accurately from the first man you meet in the street than from people who have made a lifelong and accurate study of it.
-George Bernard Shaw

What were his self-control techniques?

1. Avoid frustrating situations by noting when you got angry in the past.
2. Reduce your anger by taking time, focusing on other emotions (pleasure, shame, or fear), avoiding weapons of aggression, and attending to other matters.
3. Respond calmly to an aggressor with empathy or mild, unprovocative comments or with no response at all.
4. If angry, concentrate on the undesirable consequences of becoming aggressive. Tell yourself: "Why give them the satisfaction of knowing you are upset?" or "It isn't worth being mad over."
5. Reconsider the circumstances, and try to understand the motives or viewpoint of the other person.
6. Train yourself to be empathic with others; be tolerant of human weakness; be forgiving (ask yourself if you haven't done something as bad); and follow the "great lesson of mankind: *to do as we would be done by.*"

Remarkable! Seneca was clear and detailed. He covered the behavioral, skills, unconscious and especially the cognitive-attitudinal aspects of self-help. He did no research; he merely observed life around him. Now, if we can add research to those ancient "clinical observations," we may be able to make more progress in the next 2,000 years. By the way, Seneca also advocated child-rearing practices and humanistic education designed to build self-esteem, model non-aggressive responses, and reward constructive non-violent behavior. Sadly, an angry political leader killed him.

Self-help methods must be tailored to each person's needs. First of all, it seems clear that we have two basic ways of dealing with our own anger. We can (a) prevent it, i.e., keep anger from welling up inside of us, or (b) control it, i.e., modify our aggressive urges after anger erupts inside. The preventative approach sounds ideal - avoid frustrating situations, be assertive when things first annoy you, eliminate irrational ideas that arouse anger, etc. But, we can't avoid all frustrations and all thoughts that arouse anger. Secondly, in the situations where we haven't as yet learned to prevent an angry reaction, we seem to fall into two easily recognized categories:

1. "swallowers " or repressor-suppressor, or
2. "exploders " or hotheaded expressers.

Do you recognize yourself and others you are close to? The "swallowers" haven't prevented the anger, they have just hidden it - suppressed it. (Don't let the fact that "swallowers" may eventually erupt in fits of rage, much like the "exploder," confuse you.) In "exploders," angry feelings and aggressive responses are immediate - little time for prevention, little time to think about avoiding anger - the emotions just spew out.

In time, we will probably have a much better classification system. But for now, the swallower-exploder distinction can help us. It seems obvious that the self-help methods of most benefit to you will depend on (a) the nature of the frustrations that still upset you (anger has not been prevented), and (b) your personality type, "swallower" or "exploder." For instance, swallowers might find certain methods, especially stress inoculation venting feelings and assertiveness, to be helpful. Exploders might use the same methods, too, but others might be more effective, e.g., self-instructions, avoiding rewards, learning tolerance, challenging irrational ideas, and strengthen your philosophy of love.

Of course, there are times when anger isappropriate and effective. Carol Tavris (1984) says anger is effective only under these conditions:
1. The anger is *directed at the offending person* (telling your friends may increase your anger).
2. The expression *satisfies your need* to influence the situation and/ or correct an injustice.
3. Your approach seems *likely to change* the other person's behavior, which means you can express yourself so they can understand your point of view and so they will cooperate with you.

If these conditions are not met, you are usually well advised to "bite your lip" or "hold your tongue" and vent your anger privately (by yourself alone), if that helps, or forget it. You will be surprised how often the suppression of hot, vile, cutting remarks avoids a nasty scene.

Both prevention-of-anger and control-of-anger methods are given in this section. The self-help methods are arranged by levels to help you plan a self-improvement project. Make use of science and your personal experience to decide what might work best for you.

Level I: Anger or aggression-control methods that focus on simple behavior and thoughts.

Reduce your frustrations.

You know who makes you mad, what topics of conversation upset you, the situations that drive you up a wall, and so on. Can you avoid them? This could be the best way to prevent anger. Even if you can't permanently avoid a person whom you currently dislike, staying away from that person for a few days could reduce the anger.

You may need to clarify or change your goals. Having no goals can be uncomfortable. Having impossible goals can be infuriating. You may need to plan ways of surmounting barriers in your way.

Reduce the environmental support for your aggression.

How aggressive, mean, and nasty we are is partly determined by the behavior of those around us (Aronson, 1984). Perhaps you can avoid subcultures of violence, including gangs or friends who are hostile, TV violence, action movies, etc. More importantly, select for your friends people who are not quick- tempered or cruel, and not agitators or prejudiced. Examples: if you are in high school and see your friends being very disrespectful and belligerent with teachers or parents, you are more likely to become the same way. If your fellow workers are hostile to each other and insult each other behind their backs, you are more likely to be aggressive than if you were alone or with tolerant folks. So, choose your friends carefully. Pleasant, tactful models are very important (Lando & Donnerstein, 1978).

Explain yourself and understand others.

It is remarkable what a difference a little understanding makes. For example, one of Zillmann's (1979) studies shows that a brief comment like "I am uptight" prior to being abrasive and rude is enough to take the sting out of your aggressiveness. So, if you are getting irritated at someone for being inconsiderate of you, ask them if (or just assume) something is wrong or say, "I'm sorry you are having a hard time." Similarly, if you are having a bad day and feeling grouchy, ask others (in advance) to excuse you because you are upset. This changes the environment.

Develop better ways of behaving.

Although we may feel like hitting the other person and cussing them out, using our most degrading and vile language, we usually realize this would be unwise. Research confirms that calmly expressed anger is far more understandable and tolerable than a tirade. Moon and Eisler (1983) found that stress inoculation, social-skills training, and problem-solving methods training were all effective ways to control anger.

Try out different approaches and see how they work. Almost anything is better than destructive aggression. If you are a yeller and screamer, try quiet tolerance and maybe daily meditation. If you are a psychological name-caller, try "I" statements instead. If you sulk and withdraw for hours, try saying, "I have a problem I'd like to talk about soon." If you tend to strike out with your fists, try hitting a punching bag until you can plan out a reasonable verbal approach to solving the problem.

Baron and others (Biaggio, 1987) have shown that several responses are incompatible with getting intensely angered, i.e., these responses seem to help us calm down. Such responses include empathy responding, giving the offender a gift, asking for sympathy, and responding with humor. Other constructive reactions are to ask the offensive critic to clarify his/her insult or to volunteer to work with and help out the irritating person. This only works if your kindness is genuine and your offer is honest.

In addition to incompatible overt responses, there are many covert or internal responses you might use that will help suppress or control your anger. Examples: self-instructions, such as "they are just trying to make you mad" and "don't lose control and start yelling," influence greatly your view of the situation and can be very helpful in avoiding and controlling aggression. Indeed, one of the major methods of anger control (Novaco, 1975) uses relaxation, rational-emotive techniques and self-talk below, plus self-instruction methods.

Stop hostile fantasies.

Preoccupation with the irritating situation, including repeatedly talking about it, may only increase your anger. Also, punishing your anger-generating fantasies, substituting and rewarding constructive how-to-improve-the-situation thoughts method might work to your advantage in this case.

I am too busy with my cause to hate, too absorbed in something bigger than myself. I have no time to quarrel, no time for regrets, and no man can force me to stoop low enough to hate him **(Lawrence James).**

Guard against escalating the violence.

When we are mad, we frequently attempt an overkill, i.e., hurt the person who hurt us a lot more. There are two problems with retaliating excessively: the enemy is tempted to counterattack you even more vigorously and you will probably start thinking of the enemy even more negatively (in order to convince yourself that he/she deserved the severe punishment you gave him/her) which makes you want to aggress again. Thus, the saying, "violence breeds violence" is doubly true; violence produces more hate in your opponent and in you. Research has shown that controlled, moderate retaliation so that "things are equal" (in contrast to "teaching them a lesson") feels better in the long run than excessive retaliation (Aronson, 1984). Better yet, walk away from the argument; let them have the last word.

Record the antecedents and consequences of your anger.

As with all behaviors, you need to know (a) the learning history of the behavior (angry reactions), (b) the antecedents or situations that "set you off," (c) the nature and intensity of your anger, (d) your thoughts and views of the situation immediately before and during the anger, (e) what self-control methods did you use and how well did they work, and (f) the consequences (how others responded and other outcomes) following your emotional reaction. If this information is *carefully and systematically* recorded for a week or two, it could be enlightening and valuable. Examples: By becoming aware of the common but subtle triggers for your emotional reactions, you could avoid some future conflict situations. By noting your misinterpretations and false assumptions, you might straighten out your own anger-causing thoughts. By realizing the payoffs you are getting from your anger, you could clarify to yourself the purposes of your aggression and give up some of the unhealthy payoffs. Remember: "Aggression pays!" Perhaps you could gain the things and reactions you need from others in some other way.

Suppress or disrupt your aggressive responses, find a distraction, or use humor.

The old adages of "count to 10" or "engage brain before starting mouth" are probably good ideas. Do whatever you can to stop your impulsive aggression, like hitting or yelling. Even a brief delay may permit you to think of a more constructive response. Actually, the longer the delay the better; perhaps sleep on it or talk to a friend first. Research with children has confirmed Seneca's opinion that thinking about other things helps reduce our frustration and ire. Do something you enjoy, something that occupies your mind. Listen to music, take a bath, meditate, see a good comedy. Or use a little comedy, but it is hard to control the sarcasm.

> Lady debater: "Mr. Churchill, if I were your wife, I'd put arsenic in your tea!"
> Winston Churchill: "Lady, if you were my wife, I'd drink it."
> Abraham Lincoln, to a large lady visitor who accidentally sat on and crushed his favorite top hat: "If you'd just asked me lady, I could have told you it wouldn't fit."

Tavris (1984) says the best thing: "sometimes, to do about anger is nothing, including thinking nothing about the incident. The irritating event is frequently unimportant; its memory may soon fade away; if you stay quiet, the relationship stays civil and respectful."

When it comes to anger, you are sometimes damned if you do express it and damned if you don't. Swallowing anger may be unwise. Some theorists say that self-instructions to suppress anger for a long period of time may be risky, because it lowers our self-esteem, increases our sense of powerlessness, and increases health risks. Other theorists point to a phenomenon called "laughter in church," i.e., holding back the expression of an emotion - a laugh - may strengthen the feeling. Watch for these problems if you are holding back your feelings. If you have suppressed the emotional outburst but the anger still rages inside, you may need to vent the anger privately (#14).

He/she, who can suppress a moment's anger, may prevent a day of sorrow.

Stop using your temper to get your way, i.e., extinguish your aggression (see method #20 in Chapter 11). Several years ago, Gerald Patterson suggested that the aggressor and the victim could both be reinforced by the other. If the aggressor gets what he/she wants by making demands, threatening, yelling, calling people names, being nasty, etc., this hostile behavior is positively reinforced. But the victim who submits or gives in to these demands is also reinforced! He/she escapes the stress and stops the aggression (negative reinforcement) by letting the aggressor have his/her way. In this way, perhaps dominant-submissive or abusive relationships are maintained for long periods.

As the payoffs for your angry feelings and behavior become clear to you, try to eliminate the rewards. Example: if your anger intimidates someone into giving you your way, enter an agreement with them that they will no longer make concessions following your hostile responses. If you feel stronger, "more of a man (or stronger woman)" after being nasty, tell yourself that such a reaction is foolish, that anger is a sign of weakness not of strength, that being understanding shows more intelligence and is admired by others more than aggressiveness. Most importantly, ask the other person to help you avoid aggression by refusing to reinforce it; instead, you should be rewarded for having more pleasant interactions with them.

Record and reward better control over your temper.

Considerable research with children has shown that the consistent reward of constructive, pleasant, non-aggressive behavior (while ignoring aggressive behavior) reduces aggression and prepares the child to accept future frustrations much better. If kindergartners can learn this, why can't we as adults? Review your notes about anger at the end of each week. Note how the events seem trivial later, and how your emotions seem excessive. See if you don't find your pre-anger thoughts to be rather amusing. Start rewarding yourself for avoiding frustrating situations, for curtailing your anger responses, and for substituting more controlled, constructive responses, like empathy responses. For instance, if you dislike a relative, say a brother or a father-in-law, reward yourself whenever you increase the pleasant, interesting interactions with that person. This may counteract the conditioned negative reactions you have. See methods #3, #8 and #16 in

Chapter 11. Novaco's (1975) techniques also involve self-rewards (see #10, stress inoculation, below).

Self-punish aggression.

Like any other unwanted behavior, you can punish your own angry behavior. Also, you can *atone or over-correct or make up for* your inconsiderate behavior. But make sure this latter approach, the "let's make up; I'm very sorry" stage, isn't a con or manipulation. Many abusive persons apologize, promise it won't ever happen again, and become very loving afterwards for a while...until they get mad and abusive the next time. The idea in this method is not for you to be forgiven but to be self-punished; to make your angry aggression unprofitable and unpleasant to you as the aggressor so you won't do it again. Or You could assert yourself, and THINK about what is really making you angry and deal with the problem in a positive manner that will permit you to maintain control of yourself. You must first learn to make clear what your needs are, and how to meet those needs without hurting anyone else including yourself. Remember, vindictive acts usually end up hurting you twice as much as the original thing that angered you, and will get you into more situations that will cause you more anger to yourself. Then others will have more control over you.

Now, you can be assertive and express the things that you THINK are the things that you need and be respectful to all involved including yourself.

Let's do some more brainstorming: you should THINK about what those needs are, maintaining control of your personal remote control, use some self-calming technique as this will permit you the thought pattern to maintain control then, when you have figured out exactly what your needs and desires for the outcome are, approach the situation or person and discuss the matter with them. Use some "I" statements to keep the other person from becoming defensive. Something like "I would like to have the car repaired properly." Or "I would like it better if I could turn in my math paper corrections tomorrow afternoon." Or "I would like it better if I didn't get yelled at and called names." These types of answers need some thought and, remember, THINK. Thinking is the first part of thought, and it takes and requires thought to make good decisions and make good choices. By utilizing these things, you maintain being in control of yourself and keep possession of your personal remote control.

Chapter 15

REMOTE CONTROL
YOUR PERSONAL REMOTE CONTROL

We all have an internal **personal remote control**, just like the one for the T.V. set and VCR and stereo, etc. However, this personal remote control is built-in, and we have it with us always, unless we give it to others to push our buttons and control us. When we are beginning to get angry with someone, we are getting those personal remote control buttons pushed by the person attempting to gain control of us. As you start to stop THINKING, you are starting to hand them your **PERSONAL REMOTE CONTROL** because you are getting angry and are desiring to fulfill your personal needs without the fear of consequences. NOW!!!! If you want to maintain control of YOUR **PERSONAL REMOTE CONTROL**, you will maintain THINKING, and calculate or figure out what your personal needs are for this exact situation. OR, you could fly off the handle, forgetting to THINK, and blurt out verbally aggressive words at the person, YOU (*&(($)($)(%&), and then, what have you just done?

You handed over your **personal remote control** so they could control you instead of you controlling yourself. Just like infants do when they become angry because their diaper is dirty, they are angry at feeling dirty and their skin is irritated, and they become angry at the feeling, so their **NEED** is to have the feeling become better and their skin feel better, so the infant becomes angry and gives their **PERSONAL REMOTE CONTROL** to their caregiver, mom, dad or nanny. Why did the infant decide to give full control to someone else??? Because they couldn't do it themselves. Why didn't they just use **"I" statements**?? Because they cannot talk or couldn't accomplish the task. They also had another need, and that was they were angry that they couldn't do it themselves and required the help of another.

So, when you get angry and want someone else to entirely control the events that will follow, continue to be angry, don't think and give your **PERSONAL REMOTE CONTROL** to the other person, and they will entirely control you and the events of your life.

Let's examine the postal employee who throws mail away because they don't want to walk along the rainy streets delivering the mail. That is the first choice. They could throw the mail away in a trash bin or down a sewer, or continue to deliver it. Then, when they get caught, they become angry (at themselves for making a poor choice) at their boss who fires them immediately. Then, they make another bad choice, and decide to get even (being vindictive) and get a rifle and head straight down to the post office to shoot the place up and kill their boss. This is another bad choice; they are being controlled by their boss' button-pushing, and have given their PERSONAL REMOTE CONTROL to their boss and, eventually, the police and prison guards. This person failed to think and keep on thinking. So he goes and shoots people, and destroys, and does all of those VINDICTIVE ACTS. He gives the **PERSONAL REMOTE CONTROL** to the police who will take him into custody, stand trial, and become sentenced to prison. Then, once in prison, just like the infant that needs his diaper changed, or the two-year-old who wants and needs a glass of milk, he will succumb to the aid of the prison guards who will eagerly tell him when to get up in the morning, when to shower, when to eat, and when to go to bed at night. This mail person will have everything thought of and every control of his personal life CONTROLLED by the prison guard just like a 2- or 3-year-old. HOWEVER, since you are reading this, you must be older and more mature than a 2- or 3-year-old, and should be capable of understanding how to control YOUR PERSONAL REMOTE CONTROL and maintain control of yourself.

So, keep THINKING, keep CONTROL OF YOURSELF, keep control of YOUR PERSONAL REMOTE CONTROL, HAVE GREAT BENEFITS AND SUCCESS.

On the other hand,
You could

SUPPRESS YOUR ANGER
KEEP IT ALL INSIDE YOURSELF

Anger suppression, instead of THINKING and CONTROLLING YOURSELF, can create different problems for yourself. You could learn to use the PASSIVE-AGGRESSIVE methods of getting back at others indirectly, rather than telling them and being direct and confronting them HEAD-ON. These people whine, criticize everything, put others down, and become cynical because they haven't learned to express their needs and maintain control of themselves. This passive-aggressive manner of attempting to handle anger just doesn't work well; it leads to many unsuccessful relationships at work and at home.

Or you may just think about it forever and
Not control the situation at all.

Then you hold onto your anger, keeping it all inside of you, and your mind continues to dwell on it over and over and over until your blood pressure increases or you become so involved with this anger that you become very depressed and overwhelmed with it, and it becomes unbearable. The danger in this type of response to that need is that, if you don't control yourself and allow it to be expressed in some manner, you are on a path of self-destruction and possibly stroke from high blood pressure and other physical ailments. This type of over-thinking and not reacting can lead to not eating, depression, high blood pressure, headaches, and eventually everything will become a chore that is unpleasant to pursue. This anger will replay and replay over and over just like those instant replays on television. You could visualize it in your mind and, forgetting all the time to control yourself, figure out what your need really is and confronting the person in an appropriate manner that would allow you to vent, discuss and solve the anger issue.

Now the choice is yours to make
Do you want to be successful
Or
Not?

Some other methods that should be incorporated are recognizing that anger is a sin when manifested in a person's life that leads to harming others. The big F word (forgive) leads us to read Ephesians 4:30-32 that states in the KJV Bible, [30] "And grieve not the holy Spirit of God, whereby ye are sealed unto the day of redemption. [31] Let all bitterness, and wrath, and anger, and clamor, and evil speaking, be put away from you, with all malice: [32] And be ye kind one to another, tenderhearted, forgiving one another, even as God for Christ's sake hath forgiven you."

And
1 John 1:9[9,] "If we confess our sins, he is faithful and just to forgive us *our* sins, and to cleanse us from all unrighteousness."

And

1 John 5:14-15, [14] "And this is the confidence that we have in[2b] him, that, if we ask anything according to his will, he heareth us: [15] And if we know that we hear us, whatsoever we ask, we know that we have the petitions that we desired of him."

And

Luke 11:13, [13] "If ye then, being evil, know how to give good gifts unto your children: how much more shall *your* heavenly Father give the Holy Spirit to them that ask him?"

Also look at
Proverbs 14:17, [17]
"*He that is* soon angry dealeth foolishly: and a man of wicked devices is hated."

And

Proverbs 14:29, [29] "*He that is* slow to wrath *is* of great understanding: but *he that is* hasty[2c] of spirit exalteth folly."

And

Proverbs 15:18, [18] "A wrathful man stirreth up strife: but *he that is* slow to anger appeaseth strife."

And

Proverbs 19:19, [19] "A man of great wrath shall suffer punishment: for if thou deliver *him*, yet thou must do it again."

And

Proverbs 22:24-25, [24] "Make no friendship with an angry man; and with a furious man thou shalt not go: [25] Lest thou learn his ways, and get a snare to thy soul."

And

Proverbs 3:21, [1] "My son, let not them depart from thine eyes: keep sound wisdom and discretion."

Chapter 16

THE STORY
TEDDYBEARS TO BOMBS

At this point, we have the information to evaluate ourselves and make the decision about what we need to do for ourselves to become more successful. We have all experienced anger to the maximum at one time or another. Some people have experienced anger that has totally controlled their minds and have acted out in such aggressive manners that they have required police intervention and many other professionals to intervene to control them. This happens when we **forget to think**. Forgetting to think is a very dangerous part of anger and love. Love causes much the same physiologically and biologically related things to happen to us. It allows our endocrine system (glands) to come to our aid and rig our bodies for an encounter, whether it is love or anger. These two emotions are so strong that it usually can alter the THINKING of our minds and let others control our thoughts. As this book says in the beginning that anger is a natural and thoughtless entity within our minds that also stems from our pre-historic self, love is a learned response to our other most valuable **need** and that is wanting to be wanted by another. Just like anger, love will increase your blood pressure, make your skin flush, make your body sweat and make your heart pound like its going to outrun the fastest race car. This extreme love feeling tells our brains to dwell on one subject (just like anger does to us). Over and over in our mind is that picture, visualization of events that have happened or are planned by us to happen, to fulfill our need and only our need. As we experience this overwhelming emotional state, our minds race, and our heart pounds and we forget to **THINK.**

Like the little cartoon character with the little devil on one shoulder and the angel on the other shoulder tells the cartoon character to do something good or evil, so does the little love character or anger character tell us to **QUIT THINKING** and, when we are in this state of anger or love, we **STOP THINKING** and, when we **STOP THINKING,** we give the PERSONAL REMOTE CONTROL to the other person, allowing them full control of us instead of us controlling ourselves. And then we permit them to control all of our thinking and future lives, much like the three-year-old does. If this is the first time in love or the first time being really angry, we don't have our practice toolbox filled with appropriate responses, and are very vulnerable to the control of others so we blindly respond in whatever we have not thought about in a manner that we suppose the other person wants us to respond or what we have seen others show in our lives in the past. Again, we are being controlled by hormones and other chemicals within our bodies **WITHOUT THINKING.**

The sissy way out is to react and loose your control. It is hard, and only for the tough people to use self-control.

As we learn new skills and put them in our tool-box of skills, we actually achieve mental growth and become more independent. We usually use the tools of a child until a time when we learn that assertiveness and compromise work for us as a more mature and independent person.

Remember being a child and the psychosocial stages of development by Erickson. Let's re-look at those stages!

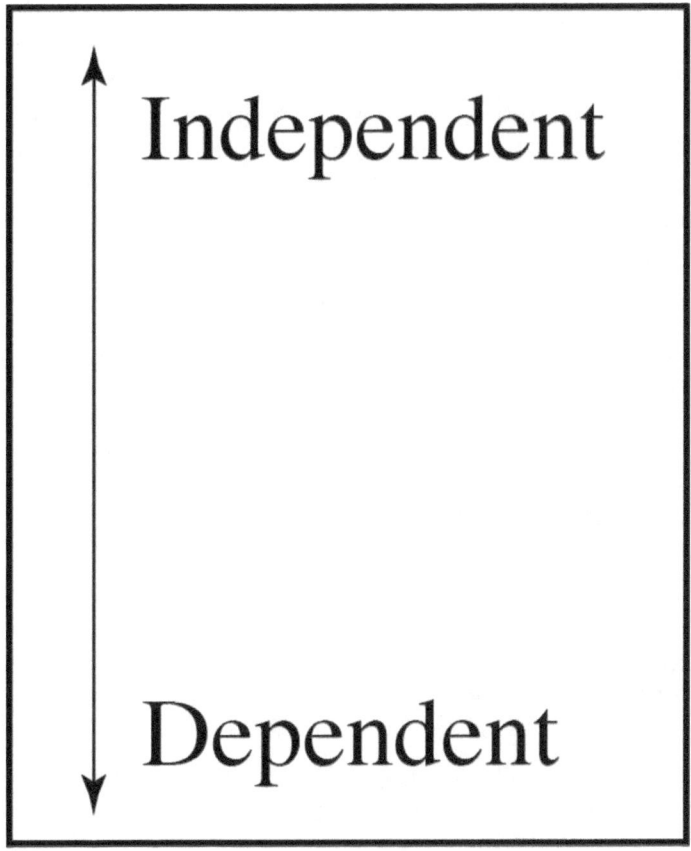

How well do you do? At each of the stages, you can go back and fix or repair them throughout life EXCEPT FOR BIRTH TO TWO YEARS OF AGE.

Early Adulthood (18-34 years)

- Psychosocial Crisis: Intimacy vs. Isolation

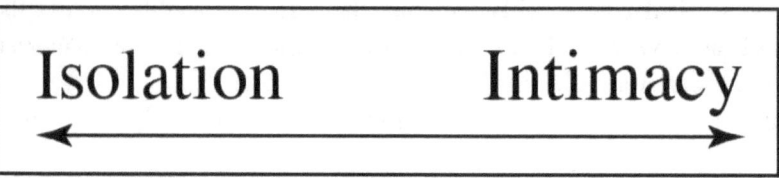

Body and ego must be masters of organ modes and of the other nuclear conflicts in order to face the fear of ego loss in situations that call for self-abandon. The avoidance of these experiences leads to isolation and self-absorption. The counterpart of intimacy is distantiation, which is the readiness to isolate and destroy forces and people whose essence seems dangerous to one's own. Now true genitality can fully develop. The danger at this stage is isolation that can lead to severe character problems.

- Central Task: Caregiving
- Positive Outcome: Form close relationships and share with others
- Ego Quality: Love
- Definition: Capacity for mutuality that transcends childhood dependency
- Developmental Task: Stable relationships; child bearing; work, etc.
- Significant Relations: Marital partner; friends.

Erikson's listed criteria for "genital utopia" illustrates his insistence on the role of many modes and modalities in harmony:

- mutuality of orgasm
- with a loved partner
- of opposite sex
- with whom one is willing and able to share a trust, and
- with whom one is willing and able to regulate the cycles

of work, procreation, and recreation so as to secure to the offspring all the stages of satisfactory development.

So, when we have physically grown up and think of ourselves as being INDEPENDENT, it is possible that we truly are not INDEPENDENT. We may back up at times of crisis and upset in our lives to those developmental stages that we didn't quite get when going through them in earlier years. And then we do it again. And again. And again. Until the time comes and we realize that this vicious circle of over and over is like a snowball getting bigger and bigger and worse and worse as we age and have more responsibilities and more serious consequences for our 2-year-old, 4-year-old or 6-year-old or 10-year- old behavior and skills that we revert back to and use.

Therefore

We must remain in control, and keep on thinking to fulfill our desires and needs. We must communicate those desires and needs with "I" statements. Like "I love the way you make me feel when I am near you", but MAINTAIN THINKING.

LOOK AT THE TEDDYBEARS TO BOMBS CHART. This non-thinking happens when your mind is all the way over to either side, at the TEDDYBEAR or at the BOMB side of the chart. The majority of the time we are using our thinking skills and moving around in the center of the chart like watching T.V. with a close friend or, on the other extreme while thinking, playing a competitive game or taking a test in school.

Most of your day is spent within the circle of living without pressure and the stress of love and anger; however, at times we tend to move toward the zone of not thinking. When you are beginning to move toward the NO THINK ZONE, you could begin to utilize your skills in your toolbox.

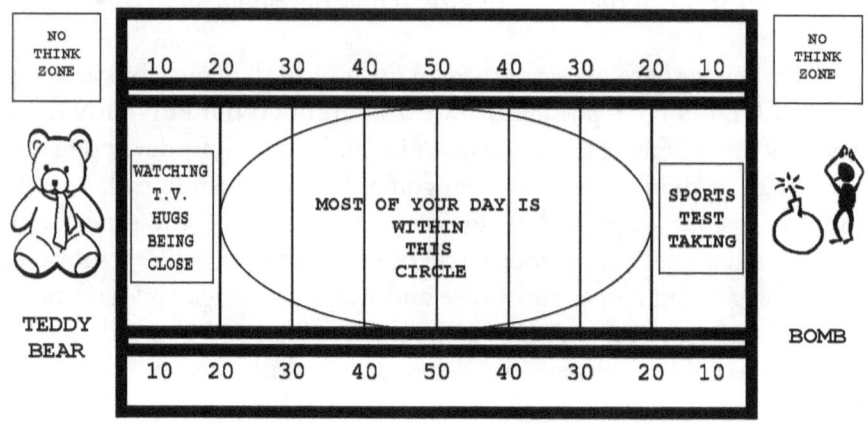

The Teddybears To Bombs Emotion Scale

Chapter 17

THE TOOL BOX

YOUR TOOL BOX SHOULD HAVE THE NECESSARY TOOLS FOR SURVIVAL AND SELF-CONTROL. By using the tools, you will remain in control of your PERSONAL REMOTE CONTROL and stop the NO THINK process. This will allow you to maintain your behavior and self-control. Keep thinking, never stop thinking.

When you begin to move closer toward anger, take a moment to THINK and feel the feelings you are having; these are all automatic, your blood pressure begins to increase, you may shake, your eyes start to jump around looking for survival things, you start to sweat, and your hair may stand up on your body.

NOW THAT YOU ARE STILL THINKING

What things are in your toolbox to help you maintain control of your feelings and thoughts? Keep thinking. I can't say that too much, keep thinking, and control all of your emotions as best that you can. Keep thinking, now! Think of possible methods to discuss your problem when you are calm. If you have to leave the area and WALK AWAY FROM THE SITUATION, DO SO NOW! but maintain control and self-calm. Here are some methods that work for others and myself:

1. Think of the TEDDYBEAR TO BOMB SCALE
2. Where are you on the scale?
3. Are you in the NO THINK ZONE?
4. MAINTAIN CONTROL OF YOUR PERSONAL REMOTE CONTROL
5. Walk away
6. Use self-talk.
7. Take a bicycle ride
8. Clear your mind
9. Exercise
10. Drink some water
11. Take slow, slow, slow, deep breaths: one, breathe; two, breathe; three, breathe; four, breathe; keep going until you are calm.

12. Stretch all of your muscles
13. Daydream; go to that wonderful place you visit in your mind.
14. Talk to a tree, wall, dog, friend
15. Maintain control of yourself

Then, when you are calm, take another slow, deep breath and THINK of possible methods to approach the person to use your "I" statements. Brainstorm those words that you may say, and THINK of the good choices and ways to deliver the message that you are angry with for a positive response.

ROLE PLAY

Yes, role play. It may sound silly to you now but, if you have a friend, mom, dad, husband, wife, or whomever, help you verbalize and set up a situation, you can practice it and learn to keep in control of yourself better than if you do not role play it.

Role play has many purposes, and we really live role play situations all through our lives. The only thing is that it is a real-life situation, and from that we learn how to adapt our anger and love emotions to each situation. Sometimes we accidentally come up with a method that works and has a positive outcome; however, many times we just revert back to our pre-historic caveperson self, and use aggression to try to overcome the opponent. And history repeats itself in our cyclical pattern over and over with the same unsuccessful way that it did the last time we used it. IF IT DIDN'T WORK THE LAST TIME, what makes you think that it will work this time????

So, have that friend role play situations with you so you can see how it feels and works. Then, reverse roles and let them be the angry one, and switch back and forth until you and your friend have seen all of the possible ways to solve the problem, and which ones are successful and positive, and that you have achieved the results that you desire and need. In fact, video tape or audio tape the whole thing to listen back when you need some uplift. Some of it may just be really funny listening to yourself using the wrong methods and acting in a DON'T THINK manner.

PRACTICE

You have used many methods that are successful in the past. Those most likely have come from practice. Most people don't get it all figured out the first time around, and it does take practice. Role play and practice are two of the main ingredients to self-control and maintaining the control over our PERSONAL REMOTE CONTROLLS. The other thing is to have many ways to think, and tools in our toolboxes. The more methods that you have in your toolbox to help you, the better you can maintain your self-control. And the more tools, the more successful you will become, and then you will eventually have the proper answers to many situations that cause you undo unrest, anger, wrong decisions and consequences that make you feel bad, make you angry, and hurt yourself.

THE KEY

One of the most important things that you can achieve now, is to THINK, control yourself, MAINTAIN CONTROL OF YOUR PERSONAL REMOTE CONTROL, and know when you are getting to the NO THINK ZONE. How can you remember to pull yourself from the area of NO THINKING and move back into the THINK ZONE? If you remain calm, and use some of the tools in your toolbox like walk away, take deep breaths, you will be able to stay in the THINK ZONE, and help yourself maintain your thought and THINKING. Practice this many times; think of all the possible things that do aggravate you, and then role play them and brainstorm the many ways that you could successfully discuss and come to a positive conclusion. Don't ever forget to THINK; it is the part of your body that regulates all of your body, and you can control all of the emotions that you will ever become exposed too! THINK, THINK, THINK.

Chapter 18
THE TEDDYBEAR TO BOMB STORY

Chapter 1

Welcome to average town

Welcome to Average Town, USA, the world where Jerry lives and attends school at an alternative school. Jerry was just staffed into this school because of his fighting and cursing with teachers and his peers.

Jerry lives with his mom, a single parent, who makes just enough to pay the bills. Jerry's dad is in jail right now for domestic battery and DUI. Jerry is very unhappy, has very low self-esteem, and is failing in school. He thinks that he has to prove to the world that he is a macho man at 15 years of age. Jerry has been arrested four times for battery on school officials, and two more times for beating up kids in his school. Jerry thinks that he is following in his dad's footsteps, and is fearful that he will have to go to jail soon, and will never amount to anything as an adult.

Chapter 2

The really cool teacher

One day, Jerry runs into a really cool teacher at school named Mr. Ed. Jerry thinks that he is kind of unusual because he talks to kids like he is one of them, and understands the trials and tribulations of being in their shoes. After a while, Jerry settled in at the new school, Mr. Ed asked Jerry: "Do you want to be a success?" Jerry replied instantly: "YES", and Mr. Ed asked him how he planned to do that with such a terrible record of dependence on other people. Jerry said that he was not dependent on others, that he was a man, and could do anything that any other man could do. Mr. Ed took him aside into his classroom, and sat him down to talk.

He said, "Jerry, I have been sent here on a special mission, to bring out the best in kids just like you, but it will take a little understanding and work on your part to become the best. Are you willing to invest a little bit of time?" Jerry said: "Sure, but what are we going to do?"

Mr. ED explained, "First we are going to go back to the beginning of your life and re-look at some growing up that you did, and then we will finally get back to today but, with a few differences, one of those being if you really want to be an independent man."

Jerry thought, boy what a goofy guy this teacher was, and what did he really mean by going back to the time when I was little??? And I really do want to become an independent man. But this school and the way it is at home isn't the way for me to do that.

Chapter 3

Skipping homeroom

A couple of days later, Jerry ran into Mr. Ed, his homeroom teacher, again as he had skipped out on homeroom a couple of times. Mr. Ed asked him, "Jerry have you thought about the challenge of becoming a man that is independent?" Jerry told him that he had been thinking more about going back to the time when he was a little kid, and wanted to know exactly what Mr. Ed meant by that?? Mr. Ed explained, "Well, Jerry, I told you that I have been sent here on a special mission - to bring out the best in kids just like you. We must first go back in your mind to the time when you were a little kid to look at how life really was and how it has progressed until now. Mr. Ed told Jerry to meet him in the homeroom classroom a half hour earlier in the morning, and he would explain more.

Chapter 4

Getting to Homeroom Early

The next day, Jerry arrived in the homeroom classroom 30 minutes early to find out what was happening. Mr. Ed was sitting at his desk drinking a cup of coffee and staring into space with a friendly look on his face. Jerry said to Mr. Ed, "Good morning. I am here, so let's get this over with". Mr. Ed told him that it wasn't going to be very fast as it has taken him 15 years, all of his life, to get to this point, and it will take considerable time to go back to the early years of his life. Jerry would need to be patient since it was Jerry who wants to learn to be independent and successful.

Jerry sat down at the desk closest to the teacher and asked, "So what now?" Mr. Ed asked Jerry to close his eyes and think of when he was a little boy growing up, and what was the first thing that he remembered. Jerry said, "That's easy. I was learning to ride a bike with my dad in the street in front of our apartment". "What else", asked Mr. Ed. He said, "It was a pretty, clear day with the sun shining down, and the bike I was riding was red with a little rust on it but it was new to me". Mr. Ed asked, "So how well did you do?" Jerry said, "I fell off a few times when dad would let go of me, and then I finally got it okay, so I could go about 50 feet pedaling as hard as I could go but, I remember now, I couldn't stop when I got to the end of the street, and I crashed." "So", Mr. Ed replied, "you were dependent on your dad or someone to help you and hold you up and help you stop". Jerry retorted, "Of course; I was just a little kid."

Mr. Ed asked Jerry to remember when he was just born, and what was that like? Jerry told him he must be goofy; nobody could remember that far back! "Well," Mr. Ed said, "Oh yes you can. Now let's just look back and think because thinking is the biggest part of gaining your independent living as a man." Jerry said, "Okay, I was just born and was screaming and crying because the doctor had smacked me on the butt." "Yep. Now you've got it, Jerry. Now, let me ask you, what did you know how to do on your own?" "Well," Jerry said, "I couldn't do anything except cry." "Why do you think you were crying, Jerry?" "Because, Uh, Um, I was angry with the doctor hitting me, I guess." "Good, Jerry, you are probably right. The first emotion that you displayed was that of anger and being mad at the doctor for hitting you. What did you do about it?" Jerry said, "There was nothing I could do; I was just born." Mr. Ed asked, "Well, since you were just born, and now you were really mad and angry with the doctor who hit you, why couldn't you do anything?" Jerry said, "Okay, I'll play your silly game. I couldn't do anything because I was dependent on anyone and everyone doing things for me, and the only thing that I really knew was to get really mad. Mr. Ed reiterated, "So, Jerry, when you were born, you only knew how to get angry and nothing else, and were totally dependent on others for everything." "Right", Jerry agreed. Mr. Ed asked Jerry to come back tomorrow morning, and discuss if Jerry remembered when he learned to use the potty or tie his own shoes, since this was a big turning point in Jerry's life. Also, he would tell him part of the secret to becoming an independent adult at that time.

Chapter 5

Learning The Secret

The next morning, Jerry arrived about 45 minutes early, as he desired the answer to the secret from Mr. Ed

Jerry asked Mr. Ed for the secret. Mr. Ed told Jerry to wait a minute because he was still thinking and drinking his coffee. Jerry sat down very impatiently, but waited for a few minutes. Finally, Mr. Ed said, "Jerry, did you think of the time when you learned to use the potty or tie your shoes?" Jerry said, "Sure I did. I asked my mom, too." He seemed very excited about sharing his story. "Mom said that, when I first used the potty chair, I was really excited and wanted to tell everyone how much of a big boy I was and how successful I had become. I told the neighbors, friends of my mom's and anyone else I could tell as I was about 2 years old and loved to tell stories about myself." Mr. Ed asked Jerry, "So, you learned to be a little more independent when you learned to use the potty, huh. And you thought that talking to friends and family was an important thing to do along with seeing them be proud of you and seeing you be happy?? Now, Jerry, did you know how to be happy and proud when you were born?" Jerry said, "I dunno. I don't think that I did." Jerry looked back into his past, and took a little mental trip with Mr. Ed. He thought about his cousin who had just been born, and only knew how to get angry when he needed to be changed or fed or something. Mr. Ed told Jerry that, when we are babies and are very dependent, we only want for us and don't really care about anyone else. We want to be fed, to be clean and dry and comfortable, and that is about it. Nothing else is a desire of a newborn infant. But, as we grow, we learn how to express being happy and loving to be with our caregiver, mom, or dad. And, little by little, we learn to love and be loved by others instead of being angry and mad at them like when we were first born. Hopefully, we learn how to accomplish love and caring along with the wonderful skill and tool of getting angry and mad."

Jerry said, "What do you mean a wonderful skill or tool of getting angry and mad? Getting mad is a good thing, Mr. Ed??, Jerry continued, Mom and Dad and my teachers and almost everyone has told me that anger and getting mad is a really bad thing, so what do you mean it is a good thing to have as a tool or skill?" Mr. Ed explained, "Well, Jerry, when you were born, for instance, you were helpless and dependent on others to help you accomplish everything that you wanted, right? How did you communicate? You could cry and ball your fists up and kick a little, showing everyone around you that you were mad at something and then, hopefully, they would figure out what you wanted by checking you out - were you wet, dirty, hot, cold, hungry, etc. When they figured it out, you learned to smile and be quiet or happy. This was when you started to learn how to love and be loved by another being, like mom or dad or some other caregiver. So, anger was a tool and skill that you had mastered by the time you were born. Now, Jerry, look at this drawing."

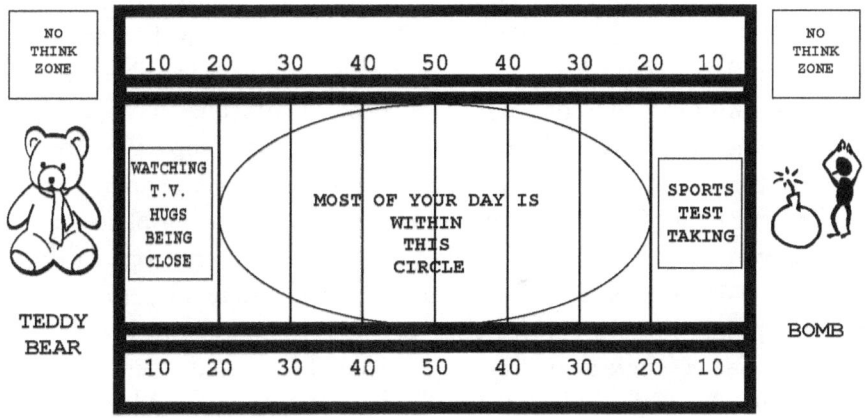

The Teddybears To Bombs Emotion Scale

"Look at where you began thinking and not thinking in the angry bomb area of this little chart. As you grew in INDEPENDENCE, you learned to love and be more teddy bear-like and, by the time you were 2 years old, you knew how to love and had an additional tool in your skills to utilize. Then, you were growing in INDEPENDENCE, as you learned to love and have friends and have your caregiver, mom or dad, respond to your loving, smiling and being happy. So, what does this mean? Well, Jerry, you had developed anger as a tool when you were dependent and, as you grew in independence, you added loving and caring as a tool or skill to use. Now, to continue growing in INDEPENDENCE, you're learning to use a variety of, or sliding scale of, loving and anger. However, to do this we must learn to stay within the THINK zone." Jerry said, "Now I am confused; what do you mean in the THINK ZONE?" Mr. Ed told Jerry to remember back when he was last very angry with others at school or at home or outside goofing off with the guys. Jerry thought for a minute and said, "Okay, I remember. I was really mad at this kid at school, and threw a desk across the room and hit a teacher that was trying to break up the fight, and the police came in and arrested me for the first time." Mr. Ed asked him "Do you think that you were THINKING at that time??" Jerry said, "Well, I don't really think so. I was mad and going to kill that stupid kid." Mr. Ed asked him, "So what really occurred?" Jerry thought for a minute and said, "I don't remember exactly; just that the police came there, and grabbed me and slapped the handcuffs on me and controlled me. Then they took me to the police station". Mr. Ed told Jerry that he had gone way past the THINK ZONE with his anger, and couldn't remember because he wasn't thinking anymore; he was in need of someone to control him just like when he was an infant and needed someone to solve the problem for him. He continued, "So, Jerry, you were acting as a dependent person needing the police in this case to take control and fix the problem for you because you weren't thinking. Now, for tomorrow, I want you to think back about situations that make you angry where you really get mad, and we will discuss how to control your personal remote control tomorrow morning. See you here at the same time okay?" Jerry said, "But I want to know now". Mr. Ed told him to think about it, and he would see him in the morning, and give him another one of the secrets.

Chapter 6

The New Secret

The next morning, bright and early, Jerry arrived in the homeroom. He was just so anxious to hear what the new secret was that he couldn't sleep all night. Mr. Ed wasn't there yet so he had to sit and wait for him to arrive. While waiting, Jerry took a sheet of notebook paper and wrote down the things that made him most angry. The list looked like this:

Things that make me mad,
by Jerry

Calling me names
Saying things about my mom or dad
Telling me I did wrong
Telling me to do something I don't want to do
Ordering me around
Sarcastic comments about me or my family Getting in my face
Yelling at me
Cursing at me
Taking privileges away
Treating me like a baby
Hitting me
Bullying me
Failing at a task
Loosing
Becoming frustrated with school work
Being caught doing wrong
Arguing with someone who doesn't understand me
Trying to control my thoughts
Trying to control my actions
Trying to make me submissive
Being told to do something that interferes with fun stuff
I want to do
Being laughed at
Being controlled
Being lied to
Not being helped when I need it

No free time

Too many responsibilities at the wrong time

Stress and pressure at school and with friends

Peer pressure

Tests at school

Mr. Ed came into the classroom just as Jerry was finishing his list and, with a loud pleasant voice, said "Good morning, Jerry. I see you have been here for a while". Jerry said, "Good morning. I want to know the new secret that you promised to tell me yesterday." Mr. Ed sat down and asked Jerry, "Do you remember what we talked about yesterday?" Jerry reiterated that they had talked about previous times when Jerry lost control and had to be controlled like a little child when he had been arrested by the police for losing his temper and punching that kid at school. Mr. EDdwent on to tell, "So you realize that you needed to be controlled because you were not in control of yourself. And that you lost your temper and control of yourself because someone had made you angry because they pushed your buttons on (YOUR PERSONAL REMOTE CONTROL)". Jerry asked, "WHAT! My personal remote control????" Mr. Ed asked to look at Jerry's list of things that make him angry. After reviewing them, he told Jerry, "These things on your list are the buttons of your Personal Remote Control. Just like the one for the T.V. set that have little buttons labeled for channel, volume, on, off, etc., only these buttons control you and only you. Most people have the same remote control buttons, too, so your's are really not unique, and you know that already because you have used those buttons to make other kids mad, haven't you?" Jerry put his head down and weakly said that he, too, had pushed other kids' buttons using some of those same tactics. Mr. Ed asked Jerry why did he push the buttons of other's?? Jerry said, "I wanted to make them mad so I could fight with them, and WIN." "AHH", said Mr. Ed, "you see, Jerry, you really are quite smart. You have learned a technique to control others when they don't want to be controlled. By Pushing Their Buttons, You Gained Control Of Them. That is a wonderful skill that you learned. Now, let's see how we can apply that research and development to your situations." Jerry was aghast - Research and development?? "You make me sound like I am a company or something." Mr. Ed said, "First Jerry, when you were born and would cry and ball your fists up because you were wet, hungry, cold, hot, or whatever, you learned how to control your caregiver by using these tools to control their behavior and fulfill your needs. As you grew up, you learned how to use the buttons on other people, like your teachers, pastor of your church, daycare person, and other kids. Once your research showed that, if you displayed some physical behavior, others would react in a certain way, almost just like you planned it for them. So, you developed a method that worked for you to obtain anything you wanted at any time that you wanted it. You pushed the buttons of others to get some benefit. Well, guess what? Jerry, you and all of your friends have come up with almost the same buttons and so have your parents and all other people in the world. Some people have other sensitive buttons that are unique to them, like a very old woman that I know who tells any little child who comes into her home that the china cabinet is off limits because it contains cherished antique glass figurines that belonged to her wonderful grandmother and, if anything would happen to anything in the cabinet, she would be crushed." Mr. Ed asked Jerry, "So what do you think her BIG BUTTON IS?" Jerry immediately responded, "her china cabinet contents." "Yep," Mr. Ed replied. "She tells everyone, if you want to get my attention and control me, you just go near or touch any of my stuff in the cabinet, and you will have total control over me. And, thus, push my buttons."

"Now, let's look at some of your buttons, Jerry.

Calling you names; what do you do when anyone calls you a name?" Jerry said, "I get mad and hit them. Mr. Ed said that Jerry would immediately hand over his PERSONAL REMOTE CONTROL to anyone who pushed his buttons. And, because they did, that would give control over himself to whomever pushed the buttons, and then they would have full control over his destiny and independence. "INDEPENDENCE?" asked Jerry." "Yes sir. You would become dependent on that person who pushed your button and lose your independence acting for their button-pushing. Would you believe that they, too, had done some research and desired to develop a method of controlling other kids in school by pushing their buttons?" Jerry hung his head, and said, "Yes, sir, I have done those same things." Mr. Ed said, "Now Jerry, what I propose is that you come up with a way that, when someone pushes your buttons, you don't react the way that they planned and, when possible, hide your buttons and remote control from everyone else. How are you going to do that? So, until tomorrow, I want you to think of methods that you can use to not REACT to their button-pushing, and remain being INDEPENDENT and in control of yourself. Jerry went off to class, and continued to think about the secret that he had learned about having a PERSONAL REMOTE CONTROL. He couldn't sleep that night and, when he would fall asleep, he would dream of nasty kids calling him names,saying things that were mean about his mom and dad, and how crummy he felt when he would become frustrated and fail at school because those were his sensitive issues and big BUTTONS that he was really affected by, just like the old woman and the glass figurines.

Chapter 7

Pushing Buttons

The next morning, Jerry arrived in class early as usual with the answers to his problem of letting people push his buttons, and that was to IGNORE THEM. Mr. Ed came into the classroom, said good morning to Jerry, and asked him what he had come up with as an answer to the big question. Jerry said, "All I have to do is ignore them." Mr. Ed told him, "Well Jerry, you're right but only partially right." Jerry got a little angry, and shouted "what do you mean only partially right? I thought about this all day yesterday and almost all night last night, and I thought of everything, and now you tell me only partially right." Mr. Ed said, "Yes Jerry, only partially right, and by that I mean, if you ignore them, what else are you going to do to finish controlling yourself and remaining independent?" Jerry thought a minute, and said, "Sorry I snapped at you. I guess you pushed my button a little on MY PERSONAL REMOTE CONTROL, didn't you, Mr. Ed?" Mr. Ed told Jerry that he had, and that it was all a part of thinking things through and looking at both sides of the equation. Jerry responded, "The equation; this sounds like math and Algebra stuff". Mr. Ed went on to tell Jerry that, when you ignore what is going on in your head, you are still angry aren't you?" Jerry thought a minute, and said, "I guess so, and what does that mean?" Mr. Ed told Jerry he had to have a method to diffuse the situation or it would continue to replay in his mind, and he could become angrier as time went on, so he would have to figure out a method to overcome those thoughts and not have them fester and become more angry. Jerry thought and said, "Uh, uh, I don't know what else I could do except maybe hit the kid, and then I would lose, and the kid would have control of my personal remote control." Mr. Ed explained, "Jerry, you could walk away from the situation, and then think of WHY did that person push my buttons and want to start a fight or argument? And then, you could figure out more methods of controlling yourself and your PERSONAL REMOTE CONTROL". Mr. Ed went on to tell Jerry methods that other successful people used like:

Walk away
Talking to yourself
Ride a bike
THINK
Be silent as silence is golden
Exercise
Whistle a tune that makes you feel good (have your
own self-song, for example: Everything is beautiful, in it's own
way LA
LA LA LA)
Listen to the wind in the trees
Go fishing
Punch a punching bag
Go for a run
Kick a tree
Laugh about it

And some people BRAINSTORM which is considering all of the things they could do even the ones that really aren't proper like:

Hitting them in the mouth
Punching their lights out
Yelling back
Pushing their buttons back

If you do this part, you must review these items and consider all of the consequences if you act that way. Like, if you punch them in the mouth, you may get arrested and go to jail, and that would be a really stupid method or solution to someone saying that you're a goof, or telling you that your pants and shirt don't match just because your pants are blue and your shirt is black.

Brainstorming is a wonderful method to use if, and I say IF, you continue and figure out or calculate all of the consequences that could follow, and scratch out the ones that cost too much. Remember, EVERYTHING THAT WE DO HAS A COST AND A BENEFIT.

When we react, we have a benefit that may cost us dearly, and be too expensive for the benefit that we receive from it. Jerry said, "This sounds like math again, Mr. Ed".

Mr. Ed said, "Jerry, let's do some role play, and I will be a kid that walks up to you and says 'Jerry you're funny looking'. What are you going to do?" Jerry said,: "I would laugh and walk away". Mr. Ed told him "Good., That would be a good method to use.", But he didn't think that Jerry would really do that just from knowing how he has seen him do things before. Jerry said, "Well, I guess I would argue with him and possibly hit him." Mr. Ed told Jerry that he was honest about it, and must think of other methods of gaining and keeping his independence and control over his PERSONAL REMOTE CONTROL and, since the bell was about to ring, he would continue this conversation tomorrow, and Jerry would figure out what to do next. Mr. Ed would help him by giving him another secret tomorrow.

Jerry went off to class, and continued to think about that simple role play situation that Jerry would end up losing and going into the NO THINKING ZONE and doing something that would have way too high a cost for the benefit.

Jerry went to class, and continued to think about what had just gone on with Mr. Ed, and what other possible solutions he could come up with for tomorrow and, also, what the secret would be tomorrow.

Jerry thought about it all night, trying to remember back to the last time when some kid said something bad about his dad being in jail, and how angry it made him, and what other possible solutions he could have used to remain in control of his PERSONAL REMOTE CONTROL.

Chapter 8
The Habit

The next morning, Jerry arrived in the classroom way early as this was beginning to be a habit, just because it was really interesting and Jerry wanted real bad to become successful and gain more control over his PERSONAL REMOTE CONTROL and himself.

Mr. Ed greeted him in a friendly voice as usual by saying, "good morning, Jerry. What did you come up with last night?"

Jerry said, good morning back to Mr. Ed, and said that he thought about what had happened yesterday when they were doing the role play and brainstormed a variety of methods that would have little if any cost and would benefit greatly, and that was to remain silent, ignore the person, and keep a log about the incident and his method of resolution. "Great," said Mr. Ed, "The journal is a wonderful method to see how well you're doing and keep track of things that you normally encounter in a day, so that you can go back and examine each one and come up with other methods to self-control."

Mr. Ed asked Jerry if he remembered the story about the "Ugly Duckling".Jerry said, "Of course I do, about the ugly little duck, and how all of the other ducks would call him names and never played with him, and kicked him out of their group, and how his parents weren't around to help him, and he went off to be alone. And one day he was a swan, and the ducks looked at him, and admired how beautiful he was, and they envied him. Mr. Ed told Jerry, "Very good. Now let's look at what really happened, and what buttons were pushed, and how the Ugly Duckling responded. The Ugly Duckling was called names, and he didn't respond; he walked away and probably used some self-talk methods of controlling his anger with the duckling acquaintances. Then he self-isolated himself, and thought about what he was going to do to remain in control of his PERSONAL REMOTE CONTROL. The Ugly Duckling remained in control, and didn't hurt or hit or say anything back to the others who were picking on him. Thus, he reduced the cost and increased the benefit for himself and became more independent. He remained alone though, and didn't have any others to support him and help him. The Igly Duckling eventually found out that he really wasn't a duck after all; he was a very beautiful swan, and could join in with other swans and have better support by their teaching and camaraderie or friendship.

"So, Jerry, you can continue to keep control over your self-control when others attempt to push your buttons by self-isolating, walking away, and THINKING about the things that have just taken place that will reduce the cost and increase your benefits. This will allow you to become more independent and in control of your PERSONAL REMOTE CONTROL. And your PERSONAL REMOTE CONTROL will not have it's buttons pushed as much every time that you don't react to others pushing or trying to push your buttons. This will let you gain in INDEPENDENCE the more you use those tools, and the kids and adults that try to push your buttons see that you have control over yourself and that they cannot control you because you have such great control. Then, eventually they will quit trying to push your buttons, and that is when you will become more successful. Now, for the big question: How are you going to remember to do all of that and remain thinking about what to use as a tool for independence and self-control?"

Jerry thought for a minute, and said that he didn't know how to not re-act and how to do that. Mr. Ed told Jerry that he would help him with the secret tomorrow.

That afternoon, Jerry thought about tying a string around his finger that could remind him or biting his tongue when he wanted to yell back at someone. But that was about all he could do. That night, Jerry couldn't sleep very well. He even dreamed about how the swan controlled himself, and thought about what the swan could have thought about. Still, Jerry didn't come up with a good method to control himself. He even thought back to when he was a little baby or a toddler, and his mother would help him control himself when he was acting poorly or messing with stuff that he shouldn't. He thought mom would hold me still in the corner for a few minutes until I got calm. Hummm, she made me stop and think!!! THINK!!! WOW, even when I was a very little kid I could THINK. So how could I progress from that help that I still require and have since I was about 3 years old. HMMM . . .

Chapter 9

Realizing

The next morning, Jerry met up with Mr. Ed in the hallway, and said that he had thought and thought, and figured out that he hadn't learned to control himself any better than what he was able to do at the age of 3 years old. He told Mr. Ed, "I haven't learned to do any self-control stuff since I was about 3 years old. I still, just a few weeks ago, needed the police to hold me still and handcuff me so that I could become calm and begin THINKING again."

Mr. Ed congratulated Jerry that he finally figured out the most important thing that he could have come up with. Jerry was shocked; he asked Mr. Ed, "What do you mean that I figured it out? I don't know anything more than when I was about 3 years old; how can that be good?"

Mr. Ed told Jerry, "Well, young man, now you have realized just how important it is to remain THINKING, and what can be done when you forget. Now we just need to work toward some tools that can help you remember THINKING is important. That is a very adult thing to remember to do, and will help you gain independence as you grow and become older. You see, all people get older just because time passes and never grow in maturity to become more independent and "SELF-ACTUALIZED". That is a term by a man named Maslow. We will talk about his theory later. And we have to do some research to figure out how to remain THINKING. You see, when we think, we can remember all of the events that bother us and make us happy. We can also plan and predict things that we want to accomplish and how those things will take place. This allows us to figure out COST AND BENEFITS of the things that will follow. But, how do we remember to THINK? We must have a game plan that, when things happen around us over which we have no control, we continue thinking and slow down to look at all of the possible solutions to the problem. And, most important, look at the other person's possible gains from this interaction and motive for saying or doing the things that have made us really angry. But, don't show them that they have made us angry at all and, as we practice these tools, we can become better at controlling ourselves. PRACTICE, PRACTICE, PRACTICE. Role-play is one very helpful method to maintain control of yourself. For the next few days, Jerry and Mr. Ed role-played different things from different points of view, just as the list of things that Jerry had developed in his list of buttons that could be pushed. Mr. Ed would play the part of the kid, and then as if he were Jerry, and Jerry would switch back and forth, too. Finally, after a few days of role-play, Jerry came to the conclusion that he had perfected methods to control himself and remain THINKING. Now Mr. Ed asked Jerry to think of the teddybear-to-bomb scale of living that had been shown to him a few days ago. Mr. Ed said, "Then, what do you think the majority of the day is like when at school or at home??"

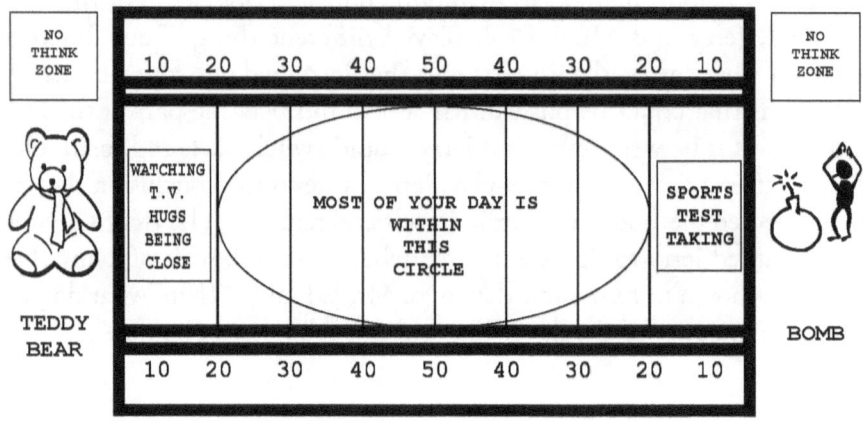

The Teddybears To Bombs Emotion Scale

"So, Jerry, let's look at the chart one more time. Keep it in your mind, too! How can you keep your mind in the thinking zone of the chart, and when are you apt to get into the NO THINK ZONE? Let's look at the chart; you can be playing football with your teammates and are more aggressive at times during the game. So, you are on the 20 yard line. If you go much farther, you will start to get mad and, if you curse out the ref, you will get benched or, if you get into the NO THINK ZONE and hit another player, you'll be kicked off the team right?" Jerry agreed that those things would take place just like Mr. Ef said that they would. Jerry said that he could control himself during games usually but it was hard, and that the thing that he thought about was the consequences, and how he would let his team down if he started not thinking and hit someone and would be benched. That had happened to him several times in practice, and the coach would send him out of the game for a little while. Jerry said, "I've got it; he sent me out so that I would remember to calm down and start thinking rationally, and then he would let me get back into the game after yelling at me for losing my cool." Mr. Ed congratulated Jerry again for coming up with the answer, and reminded him that he had told him he had all of the answers when they first met and talked about self-control and being successful.

Mr. Ed asked Jerry to think of times when he might be on the 40 yard zone and 30 yard zone and even the 50 yard zone of the teddy bear to bomb scale. And that they would talk about that tomorrow.

The next morning, Jerry had come up with some things that fit quite nicely on the scale for Mr. Ed. He met up with Mr. Ed in the classroom, and was ecstatic jumping with joy as he was making more progress he thought than anyone else could have. He showed the illustration to Mr. Ed.

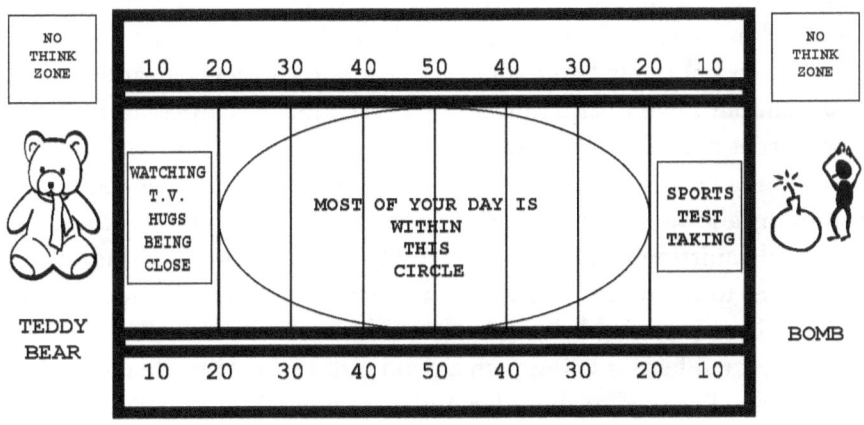

The Teddybears To Bombs Emotion Scale

Mr. Ed congratulated Jerry for an excellent job.

Mr. Ed said to Jerry, "Now let's think a little about each one of these moments, and tell me if you think some of them may float around while doing the same thing?" Jerry told Mr. Ed, "Well, I guess, uh, maybe?" Mr. Ed said, "Let me give you an example: Say the one that says chores; what is that chore?" Jerry told Mr. Ed, "Taking out the trash, cutting branches off of the tree in the backyard." Mr. Ed asked Jerry, "When you are taking out the trash and the can is full of water, or the bag rips?" "Oh! WOW. Now I see what you mean. I start to get angry, and the chore that should be just a non-emotional thing to do becomes a nasty thing to do, and I begin to get angry." "Yes", said Mr. Ed. "Or the branch you're cutting off breaks the saw blade, or the branch comes down and hits you on top of the head?" Jerry said to Mr. Ed, "I see just what you mean; then I get really angry." Mr. Ed asked Jerry to describe, paint a picture, relive that moment with him. Jerry said,: "Okay, let's see. I was taking out the trash the other day, and the can was full of water just like you said, and it was because my little sister had left the lid off of the can as usual. Now, I really got mad at the situation and my sister, too. So, I kicked the can over, which hurt my foot, and then the water ran down into my shoe getting my new sneaker wet, and put a hole into the can, too, with my foot. So I picked the can up, and threw the bag at the can, and the trash bag ripped open, and stuff spilled all over which I had to pick up and put into another trash bag. But, when I walked into the house, my wet footprints that were also a little muddy got on Mom'S new white carpet, and then Mom hit the roof and yelled at me. Then I not only had to put the trash into the new bag and into the trash can, but I had to clean my sneaker, vacuum the carpet, and use that spray carpet cleaner stuff to clean up that mess. Then Mom told me that, since I put a hole in the trash can, she would get another one and deduct it from my allowance. Man oh Man, was I really getting mad. I could feel the blood squirting in my ears, and my hands were clenched into fists. I just wanted to get even with my sister and Mom, too!" Then, Dad got home with my little sister, and she went on to show me the new doll that Dad had just gotten her for being such a good girl, and that made me madder and madder. I wanted to choke her and tear up her little stupid dumb idiot doll. So, I yelled at her about the trash can lid, and made her cry. Then, Mom and Dad jumped on me about hurting my little sister's feelings. It was like I couldn't do anything right." Mr. Ed asked Jerry, "Now let's replay that situation using the THINKING ZONE model, and retell the story about how you would do it now. Jerry told Mr. Ed, "Well, I would walk down the stairs to the backyard. Seeing that the trash can was full of water, I would take the can and gently pour out the water making sure that my new sneakers didn't get wet. And then I would place the trash in the can, and put the lid on it." "WOW!!! Mr. Ed exclaimed! "I think you can now look back and rewrite the situations, but it will take a lot of thinking to do it the first time." Jerry said, "I think that I can do it now, and I will practice each moment and each event, thinking about the possibilities before I do the action, and consider the COST AND BENEFITS before I start a move." Mr. Ed asked, "Jerry, today when you go home, I want you to write down the events that you are engaged in, and write some notes about the situations that you think about. I call this brainstorming. And then we will look at them tomorrow. okay?" Jerry went off to class, and was excited to do this new feat when he got hometo prove to Mr. Ed that he could really control and think before acting just like Mr. Edhad shown him. And, it would all be JERRY'S IDEAS, TOO!!

Chapter 10

Slipping

That afternoon, Jerry got into a little mess at school when a kid bumped into him in the hallway. Jerry pushed him, and the teacher wrote him up on a referral. Then, when Jerry got home, his mom looked at his daily progress sheet, and sent him to his room. Then Jerry pushed his radio/CD player onto the floor, and his mom jumped down his throat telling him that he was going to have to write sentences for those actions. So Jerry ran out of the house and over to his friend's house where he stayed until after dinner. Then his mom sent him to his room with a bologna sandwich instead of lasagna that the rest of the family had for dinner;and that was his favorite. Jerry remembered what he was supposed to work on for Mr. Ed, and thought this would be a wonderful time to start writing about the things that went on. So, Jerry wrote and BRAINSTORMED about all of the things that were going on in his mind and how angry he had become and who really got punished for doing the wrong things. Jerry came to the conclusion that one of the things that started it all was the kid accidentally hitting his arm that made the books fall, and he didn't think before he pushed the other kid. So he DIDN'T THINK; uh, huh; he had acted on instinct, or uh, he REACTED instead of acting and thinking. Then when, he got home, his mom sent him to his room (a reminder to think), and he started listening to his CD player. His mom came in and turned it off. Then he further hurt himself by pushing it onto the floor, and now will have to purchase another one out of his allowance that he had to save for 2 months to purchase it in the beginning. And then, instead of lasagna for dinner, he had a crummy bologna sandwich, and further punished himself. He then feverishly wrote down the cost and benefits, and came to the conclusion that there were no benefits and lots of costs, so he had earned and worked toward a ZERO.

The next morning, he went over to Mr. Ed's classroom, and told him all about what had happened. They both went over some alternatives that Jerry had come up with so that, in the future, Jerry would maintain control and keep THINKING.

Chapter 11

Helping Others

The next night, Jerry's girlfriend had a fight with her mother, and went to Jerry's bedroom window around 11:00 P.M. Jerry ran off with her, and stayed out almost all night instead of thinking and staying at home. Jerry was out all night long and, when he had to go to school, he was really worn outand could hardly keep his eyes open during school. Then his teachers kept riding him telling him to do his work and stay on task. The principal called his mother to tell her that Jerry needed more sleep as he was just worn out and could do almost none of his school work. Jerry's mom intervened and asked Jerry why he was so terribly tired since he was grounded to his room because of the previous episode.He was honest, and told the story about his girlfriend, and that they were chased home by the police because they were out at 4 o'clock in the morning. Now Jerry had more consequences, and was still batting a ZERO.

Mr. Ed asked Jerry what he intended to do to keep in the THINKING ZONE? Jerry told him that it was a really hard thing to do but, with all of these events written down, he should be able to make better choices now.

The next night, Jerry had a good evening, and thought about all of the things that he was supposed to do before doing them, and set himself up to WIN AND WIN BIG. Jerry took the trash out, emptied the water out of it, gently placed the trash bag in the can, and wiped his feet upon entering the house. He said something nice to his little bratty sister, and was even helpful when she needed help with her math for school. He showed her how to subtract using her fingers again for the hundredth time. His girlfriend came to his bedroom window at 10:30 P.M., and said that she had a fight with her mother again and, since they didn't get into that much trouble the other evening, wanted him to go out with her again. But, this time, Jerry said to come over to the door and come in. Then Jerry went to his mom and asked her to help with the problem that his girlfriend was having. Mom sat quietly and listened to the whole story, and then said that she would call Sally's mom and talk to her, and tell her that Sally was at their home so that they wouldn't worry either. And, by 11:00 p.m., everything was worked out, and Jerry went back to his room and went to sleep. He told Mr. Ed that he had been successful, and the biggest thing that had happened was that he used the adult thinking that his mom possessed, and he maintained being in the THINK ZONE. He really felt good about performing this task like an adult, and later, when he talked to Sally, she was very happy that Jerry's mom had helped, too, and now she and her mom aren't fighting as much anymore.

Chapter 12

The Success Gang

NOw, Mr. Ed introduced Jerry to the rest of the SUCCESS GANG, and let him join in their success, too. They welcomed him, and told him that at school, since he was one of the group, they, too, would ride him and help him, and give him support, and even take phone calls from him to help him stay in the THINK ZONE, and he, too, could become a very successful goal-oriented kid like they were.

A few weeks later, Mr. Ed ran into Jerry in the hallway. Jerry had to tell Mr. Ed that it was really working, and that he continued to use the same TEDDYBEARS TO BOMBS scenario as the others in the group used. They were really becoming great friends, and helped him to stay a successful kid.

Some of the kids even helped him with his algebra and, at the end of the school year, the principal was standing on the stage in front of all of the teachers and students, and announced that, out of all of the students, there was one who had made such outstanding progress in attitude, sports and academics.He was giving the outstanding student scholar award to Jerry. Jerry stood in front of the school and accepted the award, and told his story about how the SUCCESS GANG had been the ones who helped, and that Mr. Ed was the one who had made him realize that Jerry had to maintain control of himself or someone else would. And Jerry thanked Mr. Ed and the students who were part of the Success Gang.

Keep practicing and using new appropriate tools to add to your skillbox or toolbox, and then you, too, can and will become more positive, have higher self-esteem and more independence. Keep in mind that you can pass this skill on to others, and help them learn that there are more ways to become prosperous, independent, successful and become the real person who was meant to be.

REFERENCES

Erikson, Erik H. Childhood and Society. New York: Norton, 1950.

Erikson, Erik H. Identity and the Life Cycle. New York: International Universities Press, 1959.

Sheehy, Gail. Passages: Predictable Crises of Adult Life. New York: E. P. Dutton, 1976.

Stevens, Richard. Erik Erikson: An Introduction. New York: St. Martin's, 1983.

(Novaco, 1975)
Carol Tavris (1984)

(Biaggio, 1987)
Moon and Eisler (1983)
Zillmann's (1979)
(Lando & Donnerstein, 1978)
(Aronson, 1984)

-George Bernard Shaw
Hans Toch (1983)
(Nagler 1982)
(Wile, 1993; Maslin, 1994)

Jampolsky (1985)
Johnson and Goodchilds (1976)
Maslow (1971)
(Fullerton, 1977)
Potter-Efron & Potter-Efron (1995)

http://mentalhelp.net/psyhelp/chap7/chap7c.htm#a
(Derlega and Janda, 1981)
Konrad Lorenz (1966)
Spielberger (1988)
(Maslow, 1972)

http://www.self-esteem-nase.org/
THE TRUE MEANING OF SELF-ESTEEM

by Robert Reasoner
University of Illinois at Urbana-Champaign
Counseling Center

University of Illinois at Urbana-Champaign

(Endnotes)
[1.] *The Holy Bible : King James Version.* electronic ed. of the 1769 edition of the 1611 Authorized Version. Bellingham WA : Logos Research Systems, Inc., 1995, S. Ps 139:13-15

[II.] *The Holy Bible : King James Version.* electronic ed. of the 1769 edition of the 1611 Authorized Version. Bellingham WA : Logos Research Systems, Inc., 1995, S. 1 Jn 1:8-9
in: or, concerning

[III.] *The Holy Bible : King James Version.* electronic ed. of the 1769 edition of the 1611 Authorized Version. Bellingham WA : Logos Research Systems, Inc., 1995, S. 1 Jn 5:14-15

[iv] *The Holy Bible : King James Version.* electronic ed. of the 1769 edition of the 1611 Authorized Version. Bellingham WA : Logos Research Systems, Inc., 1995, S. Lk 11:13

[v.] *The Holy Bible : King James Version.* electronic ed. of the 1769 edition of the 1611 Authorized Version. Bellingham WA : Logos Research Systems, Inc., 1995, S. Pr 14:17
[c] hasty...: Heb. short of spirit

[vi] *The Holy Bible : King James Version.* electronic ed. of the 1769 edition of the 1611 Authorized Version. Bellingham WA : Logos Research Systems, Inc., 1995, S. Pr 15:18

[vii] *The Holy Bible : King James Version.* electronic ed. of the 1769 edition of the 1611 Authorized Version. Bellingham WA : Logos Research Systems, Inc., 1995, S. Pr 19:19

[viii] *The Holy Bible : King James Version.* electronic ed. of the 1769 edition of the 1611 Authorized Version. Bellingham WA : Logos Research Systems, Inc., 1995, S. Pr 22:24-25

[ix] *The Holy Bible : King James Version.* electronic ed. of the 1769 edition of the 1611 Authorized Version. Bellingham WA : Logos Research Systems, Inc., 1995, S. Pr 3:21

[x] *The Holy Bible : King James Version.* electronic ed. of the 1769 edition of the 1611 Authorized Version. Bellingham WA : Logos Research Systems, Inc., 1995, S. Pr 14:29

www.ingramcontent.com/pod-product-compliance
Lightning Source LLC
Chambersburg PA
CBHW051450280526
45785CB00003B/1500